MY LIFE I DECIDE

Rinku Sawhney is a social impact entrepreneur, personal excellence and mind-shift coach, and a TEDx Speaker. She is the founder of Elevated Minds, a startup committed to motivating people to achieve new heights in life. Her workshops and trainings have helped people gain clarity and identify roadblocks in their path to success. An alumnus of IIM-Bangalore, Rinku started her career in the IT industry and soon after decided to become a life coach. She has devised 'The Success Framework' programme which is aimed at achieving holistic growth and personal excellence of individuals. *My Life I Decide* is her first book.

MY LIFE I DECIDE

19 Thought-provoking Ideas to Change Your Life

RINKU SAWHNEY

PAN

First published 2019 by Pan
an imprint of Pan Macmillan Publishing India Private Limited
707, Kailash Building
26 K. G. Marg, New Delhi – 110 001
www.panmacmillan.co.in

Pan Macmillan, The Smithson, 6 Briset Street, London EC1M 5NR
Associated companies throughout the world
www.panmacmillan.com

ISBN 978-93-89109-24-5

3 5 7 9 8 6 4 2

Typeset in Adobe Jenson Pro by Manmohan Kumar

Printed and bound in India at Repro India Ltd., Mumbai

To the limitless greatness that lies within you. Let it unleash.

CONTENTS

FOREWORD

I met Rinku Sawhney through LinkedIn, and her title description drew me to further explore her profile. It said: Social Entrepreneur, Culture Creator, CXO Coach and Transformation Catalyst.

What really fascinated me most about her was her interest in storytelling. Storytelling has enthralled me all my life. As a little boy, I would be mesmerized with the tales that my grandfather and my widely travelled father would narrate to me. And this legacy of storytelling I have passed on to my children as well. On most occasions, I have intuitively employed the skill of storytelling to put forward my thoughts and have been told that the impact is deeply inspiring.

I don't believe that stories come from just reading books or listening to others. Many of these stories come from observing people in everyday life, and some of them leave a painful impact on you. Which is why these days I tell my protégés that I keep my failures closer to me than my successes.

Rinku has experienced a lot in her life. One afternoon when I met her along with Vipin, her husband – who serendipitously turned out to be my ex-colleague – I was fascinated with her journey and indomitable spirit. Her resilient mind has made her rise above her sometimes demoralizing physical ailments and made her what she is today. She is a strong woman with a tender heart and someone who is immensely gifted with a unique emotional intelligence. Her frailty belies her resolute will and her fierce desire to be a 'transformation agent'.

In this book, Rinku has broken down the complicated ideas that plague each one of us into simple steps. She has made it easy for readers to both grasp the issues that hold us back in life and implement the remedies to overcome them. She instils in us the greatest quality that is required of us – self-belief. In that itself I believe lies the panacea for all ills. She urges you to explore your innate abilities and unleash your potential.

A must-read book and a door that takes you towards these priceless life lessons.

Sandip Das
Independent Board Director and Advisor,
Sterlite Technologies Limited

INTRODUCTION

There are some people who seem to possess the 'Midas touch', an almost magical ability to achieve all their dreams. Success seems to follow them as nonchalantly as if it were their shadow. So, what is their secret? What distinguishes them from all the remaining people who are struggling to achieve the ever-so-elusive 'success'? If we were to decode the one key characteristic that makes these people successful, it would be that they have chosen to expel the 'Secret Saboteur' from their systems.

What is a Secret Saboteur? How does it impact someone's system? And most importantly, what is this system?

The system I talk about is our *mind*, the workshop where all our dreams come to life. We are told that our mind is nothing less than a miracle; it can create the life we want. If that is true, why do most of us end up struggling? Why do we feel like the circumstances in our lives are not in our control and that external factors are dominating our lives? How can we make this extremely powerful and miraculous 'mind' work in our favour? Why are we unable to live and create the life that we want? Can we really make our 'mind' help us realize all our dreams?

These are intriguing questions. What I have understood from my own experiences and my experiences as a coach is that the reason we are unable to live the life we desire is because we do not know how our mind works and why it is not helping us create the success we want: There is a demon inside us, which I call the 'Secret Saboteur', blocking and sabotaging our success. Whenever we dream of accomplishing a long-cherished idea, before our powerful mind can even start working on it, the saboteur intervenes, in the form of our introspective self-talk, and starts dissuading us:

What if you fail?

You really are not good enough. What makes you think you can create something as big as this?

Remember how you lost all your savings when you tried the last time. History will repeat itself, so stop acting like a fool.

You are too small and unfit for this. It's out of your bounds. Do you live in a fantasy world?

The Secret Saboteur poses these questions in your mind and even before you can begin, your mind becomes doubtful and you therefore never act in the direction of your success. If you haven't accomplished your desired goals yet, ask yourself: Why not?

It's all because of Mr Saboteur.

Let us understand how Mr Saboteur gets accommodation in our minds. Renowned revolutionary molecular biologist and former professor of medicine at Stanford University, Dr Bruce Lipton explains that our mind has two parts: the conscious and the subconscious.[1] 90 per cent of our adult mind is the subconscious and the remaining 10 per cent is the conscious part. The conscious mind is the part that thinks, logics, analyzes, and decides. It is the rational and objective mind. All our desires, wishes, and aspirations reside here. Then there is the subconscious mind within which reside all our paradigms, belief systems, thought patterns, and habits.

However, when a child is born, there is no separation between the conscious and the subconscious mind. Till approximately eight years of age, the child's mind does not attain conscious functioning.[2] So during these years, the subconscious records everything and anything that is presented to it, no questions asked. The mind is like a blank canvas, and then the canvas starts filling up with voices that belong to our parents or guardians, friends, teachers, the environment, which includes our culture, religion, community, country and the people we meet on a day-to-day basis. These voices, which are essentially rules for surviving and succeeding, passed on from generation to generation, live in our subconscious mind and form our life's blueprint. How many times have we heard statements like:

'It's better to be safe than sorry,'

'Life is hard,'

'You can never become a millionaire',

and so on.

Each of these voices creates a virtual, invisible limit in our mind, which we cannot exceed. Before we realize, an invisible portable box is created, holding us captive. This blueprint starts determining how we perceive the world and ourselves. Our beliefs about what is possible and what's not, what we should do and we shouldn't, what is achievable and what is not, what is right and what is not, what is acceptable and what is not, gets dictated by this blueprint.

The subconscious mind's job is to create a reality out of these recorded preconceptions. It is the irrational mind, which like a CD player, simply plays what has been recorded. Science has found that in our regular life, only 5 per cent of our behaviour comes from the conscious mind; 95 per cent of our life comes from the subconscious mind. So, if you have negative programming, 95 per cent of the times you will create negative experiences in your life.

Let us understand this with a few examples.

You read a highly motivational self-help book and you feel encouraged to change your life. But how many lives have really changed after reading these books? Of course, a minuscule number. Why? Because it's the conscious mind that reads the book and is ready to change, but not the subconscious mind. So our life remains the same.

When it comes to exercising, the conscious mind knows and understands that it is beneficial for our health and would help us attain a fit body and facilitate weight loss; but in most cases, the subconscious mind associates exercise with pain, and so we witness many people keep postponing their exercise routine. They consciously know that eating right and exercising will help them get fitter, but they still don't commit to it. It is because subconscious mind is at play here.

If you have been constantly exposed to negative ideas and environments while growing up, you will end up creating the same reality for yourself.

The ideas or conceptions, which give you a not-so-hopeful view of the world and force you to demoralize yourself – in other words, self-sabotaging notions – give birth to the Secret Saboteur.

Now, since our subconscious forms 90 per cent of our mind as opposed to the 10 per cent of the conscious mind, it is like imagine ten equally strong people fighting in tug of war, where nine people are on one side, against one person on the other side. Obviously, nine people end up winning every time. And this is the reason why ultimately we lose to Mr Saboteur.

Earlier, we discussed the key element that sets apart all successful people from the rest, which is, the subtle art of ejecting Mr Saboteur. When there is no Saboteur sitting in your 'All Powerful Mind', you will be easily able to work towards your success. Narendra Modi, Amitabh Bachchan, Sachin Tendulkar, Virat Kohli, Saina Nehwal, and so many others are legends because they have learnt the art, the skill of ejecting Mr Saboteur. I call this skill: *Mastering the Self*. This is the skill I will train you as we begin this amazing journey.

Another reason we end up jeopardizing our success is that we do not understand the mechanisms of this universe. There is a certain resonance between how our minds work and how the universe operates. You get back what your mind puts out, like a boomerang. You throw it out and it comes back to you.

When I was first introduced to this idea, honestly I too was sceptical. How was it possible that our minds and the universe are aligned? I wanted to test all these theories.

This was the period when I was going through innumerable health issues; issues that had even the doctors puzzled. They could not figure out what was wrong with me. I went through a barrage of tests, and all the results seemed fine, yet I was unwell most of the time. I tried all possible treatments, conventional as well as alternative, but all was in vain. So much so, that I had lost all hope of regaining my health.

Then I decided to test this new concept that I had stumbled upon. I first started with the idea that we attract whatever our dominant thoughts are. So, if our thoughts are predominantly negative, we will attract and experience more negativity; if we have mostly positive thoughts, we will attract and experience positivity.

So, I made a conscious and deliberate effort to think positively whenever I caught myself being negative. It was not easy, as this behaviour was a part of my subconscious exercise. But this was my only hope to cure myself. So, I made an effort to change my way of thinking. I also started visualizing myself as a healthy and happy person every night before going to sleep. I kept this up for a couple of weeks and could not see any results. But I refused to give up. I was determined to make it work. There were times when I thought '*All of this is rubbish*'. But something inside me kept pushing me and inspiring me to continue. And then the anticipatable happened. My health gradually started improving. I felt more energetic and active than ever before. I started looking a lot younger than my age. People started complimenting me for my energy and youthfulness. This was proof for me that our minds and the universe work together to change and uplift our lives.

This experience gave me the confidence to share these invaluable insights with the world. My journey of becoming who I am today started with this intention. Based on the knowledge that I had acquired and applied on myself, to test these concepts, I started working on systems and methodologies that are outcome-driven and can help one overcome their blocks.

In each chapter, I share stories of my clients or participants I have met at my workshops. These are people who have created miracles in their lives by following these simple yet life-changing ideas.

The first part of the book: Fight the Secret Saboteur, identifies the various weapons used by the Secret Saboteur and details techniques to defeat him in each case. Each chapter in this section unravels a destructive hidden weapon of Mr Saboteur and then helps you understand how it's jeopardizing your life. There are exercises, strategies, and tools in each chapter that will help you fight and destroy all these weapons.

The second part: Take Charge, focuses on all the attributes, qualities, and characteristics that will facilitate you to slide into the driver's seat of your life and take complete control of it. The strategies shared in these chapters are based on real experiments. These simple tools if practised consistently, will give you desired results. Every idea shared in this part shows you how to become the master of your life and drive it on your own terms and expectations.

The final part of the book is called: Food for Thought. Here, I share some ideas that will act as catalysts to this incredible journey of transforming your life.

The nineteen ideas shared in this book are akin to perfectly honed tools. They will disrupt the usual patterns of your thinking and behaviour that restrict you. They will help you unravel the very core of who you truly are and who you want to become. One thing is guaranteed: if you implement them in your life, you will see your life changing for good.

Your mind is your best friend and secret weapon to create unprecedented success in your life. All we need to do is learn the art of mastering it – and this is exactly what this book will help you accomplish.

'The mind is everything. What you think you become.'

– The Buddha

I

HOW TO FIGHT THE SECRET SABOTEUR

1

THE POTENCY OF QUESTIONS

Do questions hold you back or take you forward? Most of us are clueless about the role that questions play in our lives. The quality of questions that we ask others and ourselves has a direct impact on the quality of our life, be it personal, professional, or spiritual. Harnessing the power of questions is a complete game changer.

Questions are the most powerful way to reach solutions. It has been scientifically proven that our brain automatically starts looking for solutions to questions as soon as we ask them. It continues working on them in the background, even when we are not aware of it. Questions trigger the brain and get our creative juices flowing. They encourage us to take a more exploratory approach, which tends to foster a completely new set of insights.

When my son was around four or five years old, like any other kid, I remember, he used to endlessly ask questions. He was so inquisitive that we used to fondly call him, 'Question Mark'. It's not just him, all children are naturally curious when they start exploring the world; they want to know everything that seems mysterious to them. Curiosity is a sign of creativity. As children, we are all extremely curious and hence creative, but this curiosity gradually diminishes as we grow older and get caught up in our life's challenges.

Asking questions to self or to others is an inherent human quality, but as we grow, the quality of these questions plummets. Now, this is the first weapon used by Mr Saboteur, driving us to ask lousy questions. Our questions look something like:

Why am I not pretty or handsome like my favourite actor?
Why can't I lose weight?
Why can't I be successful?
Why does this always happen to me?

Now, the task of our brain is to find answers to our questions. So the brain will start searching for answers to these questions. What do you think could be the answers? You are not pretty because you are not good enough. You can't lose weight because neither exercising nor dieting works on you. You can't be successful because you are a failure. And so on and so forth.

These questions obviously do not come from curiosity. These are disempowering questions and therefore elicit demoralizing answers. There is little scope left for the brain to trigger the creative centres of the brain when we ask such questions.

To defeat this weapon of the Secret Saboteur, we need to get into the habit of asking great questions, which I call 'solution-based questions'. The brain will then start looking for solutions and trigger creativity. Let us look at some solution-based questions:

What efforts can I take to improve my work?
How can I balance my personal and professional life?
How can I improve my health?
What do I need to do or become to be successful?
What are these repetitive events trying to teach me?

Because the brain needs to provide solutions, it triggers the grey cells or the creative centres inside it to look for answers, which will lead us to our desired outcomes.

For example, when you ask the third question – 'How can I improve my health?' – your brain will start looking for an answer, trigger the creative circuits, start exploring, and you might just stumble upon an old friend who is a fitness trainer who can help you with your health and fitness. It might seem like a coincidence, but it is your brain doing all the magic.

'You can tell whether a man is clever by his answers. You can tell whether a man is wise by his questions.'

– Naguib Mahfouz

This is such a reflective quotation. The quality of the questions you ask yourself and others speaks volumes about your character. It shows who you are and where you are headed to.

Asking solution-based questions is the most effective way to approach any problem. Questions are a great way to stimulate creative thinking in any field, be it teaching, business, or the corporate world. If used skilfully, it can give tremendous results. If teachers started asking questions like:

What do you think will happen if I change this angle by one degree?
What would happen if there was no atmosphere?

It would encourage the children to think creatively and enter the explorative mode. Similarly, in a corporate scenario, when leaders ask questions such as: '*What do you think should be done?*', it encourages employees to start thinking creatively. When people are encouraged to get creative, the outcomes they produce are nothing less than outstanding.

Suresh was always dissatisfied. In my conversations with him, it was clear to me that he suffered from a mild form of depression. Even if there was a clear reason to be happy (such as his recent promotion), he said he still felt low. Of the many exercises I gave him, the one that proved to be the most effective was – any guesses? – to ask *questions*. I gave him a list of questions and told him to ask them to himself whenever he felt low. When he read the list, I could see irritation on his face. He clearly found the entire exercise preposterous.

'How will these questions help me?' he would grumpily ask me.

I said, 'If you trust me, do as I say. However, there is only one condition: None of the answers should be "nothing". If you feel like the answer is "nothing", replace it with something that might not be true right now but is affirmative.'

After about a month, he met me and I could see an obvious change in his demeanour.

'Wow, that's the first time I've seen a smile on your face. Keep that on always,' was my first reaction.

He shared that the exercise with questions had worked magically for him and after applying the affirmative answers on himself, he felt like a completely new person.

'I feel good and happy for no reason now,' he told me.

I am sharing the list of questions here as my aim is to provide solutions to people. They might seem basic, but they have helped in making massive transformations in people.

How can I make myself happy?
What am I committed to creating in my life? How will I feel when I get there?
How do I look when I smile?
How do I feel when I smile?

What am I excited about right now?
What am I happy about in my life right now?
What am I grateful for in my life right now?
What is great about me right now?
What am I proud of about myself?

Once, during one of my seminars, a participant asked me, 'How can one stay motivated all the time?' My answer was, 'You just have to ask yourself powerful questions every day.'

Yes, questions have the power to keep us motivated. They have the power to inspire us to take action. It is also a brilliant strategy to use *the power of questions* when setting goals. We all know about SMART goals (Specific, Measurable, Attainable, Relevant and Timely). They are certainly a powerful way of setting and accomplishing goals. However, if we couple them with solution-based power questions, it becomes a potent combination. Say, for example, you have a SMART goal: 'My enterprise will achieve a 300-crore turnover by December 20xx.' Now, couple it with questions like:

How shall I achieve the target of a turnover of 300 crore in the next three years?
What expertise and resources would I need to make this possible?
What steps do I need to take to make this possible?

You will be amazed at the speed with which you will start seeing results.

Asking right, powerful and solution-based questions is an art and a success-habit, which can be mastered with conscious and deliberate practice. Every successful person has a habit of asking great questions.

> ***'If I had an hour to solve a problem and my life depended on the solution, I would spend the first 55 minutes determining the proper question to ask, for once I know the proper question, I could solve the problem in less than five minutes.'***
>
> ***– Albert Einstein***

How profound is this statement!

The first idea that you need to imbibe on this journey is to silence the Secret Saboteur by developing the art of asking – yourself and others – great questions. It is one of the most powerful and fundamental ideas on this journey. All the chapters that follow are about using this art. I shall be asking you a lot of questions throughout the book, so keep your writing pads ready and note down the insights that you might come upon during this journey with me. Who knows what might turn out to be a life-changing breakthrough? So, are you ready to begin this journey!

2

THE UNSTOPPABLE POWER OF DECISIONS

The choices we make have consequences.

Do you know that every single decision you make at any point has tremendous power to influence and even change your entire life?

When we hear the word 'decisions', the first thought that comes to our mind is big, important decisions regarding: business, career, marriage, financial and other major issues. These are undoubtedly important and life-changing decisions. But we do tend to overlook the fact that we make innumerable decisions in our lives every day. It would not be an exaggeration if I were to say that everything we do or say or think or feel is a decision. What time we get up every morning is a decision. What we wear for work is a decision. What we eat for breakfast is a decision. How we choose to feel and behave every day, every moment is also a decision. What we choose to endure and tolerate in our lives is also a decision.

One of the most destructive weapons of the Secret Saboteur is the way it influences our decisions. This reminds me of a childhood friend, Shubhangi, whom I had not been in touch with after school. One day, we bumped into each other in a mall. It was a pleasant surprise! However, I felt like she did not seem to be delighted to see me. I insisted that we go to a café and chat for a few minutes. She seemed a little hesitant to accept my request, but she could not say 'no'.

I wondered what was going on in her life. I could sense that something was definitely not right with her. During our school days, Shubhangi used to be a jolly and flamboyant girl.

Initially, she seemed uncomfortable talking to me, and before I could start conversing with her I began by making her feel secure and at ease. She wore her sunglasses even inside the café. I requested her to remove them, but she was reluctant.

While we waited for our coffee, we chatted about everything from our pasts to the present. After a while, I nonchalantly asked why she kept wearing her sunglasses even we were when inside the cafe. She avoided the question and indifferently said that she had an eye infection. I was not convinced by her answer and my concern was starting to grow. I asked her about her family. She told me that she had been married for fourteen years and had two daughters. One was twelve and the other ten. And she had been a homemaker.

From the outside, everything seemed great, but my instincts told me that all was not well as much she was trying to make it look healthy. I could see some bruises on her arms, which made me highly suspicious of something not being right with her. I could not hold myself anymore and driven by my overwhelming concern for her, I impulsively reached out and removed her sunglasses. Both her eyes were swollen and had marks around them. I was shocked.

'Who did this to you, Shubhangi?' I asked.

'No, it's nothing. I just fell down from the stairs,' she lied.

'Oh, please. Who are you trying to fool? I know what these bruises are. Just tell me. Who did this?' I enquired.

After a lot of insistence, she finally told me that her husband would beat her regularly.

'So, you have been suffering his rash behaviour for the last fourteen years? Why?' I could feel the anger surging inside me.

'No, no. He has anger issues, that's all. He says sorry later, and trust me, Rinku, he really means it. Otherwise, he is quite an understanding husband. He takes good care of our daughters and me,' she tried defending him.

'I don't believe this, Shubhangi. What happened to your independent and headstrong spirit? You always fought for justice, even in small matters at school. How come you have changed so much? What makes you think that your husband is understanding? Someone who is so violent and merciless – how can you defend him?'

'What am I supposed to do? Tell me. Divorce him and live with the stigma of being a divorcee. You know how our society treats divorced women. Plus, how will I bear the expenses of a legal battle with a man like him? I have two daughters. How will I secure their lives? Where will I get my finances from? I'm just a homemaker.' She was now hysterically crying.

I let her cry first and feel relaxed. Then I said, 'Shubhangi, when did you start believing that you need a man as a shield? And what kind of shield is this man, who is no less than an animal? And do you think your children are not in agony right now, seeing you in this state? Do you think you and your girls don't have the power to create a great life together? What makes you believe that you and your girls are so powerless?'

'Then tell me. What should I do?' She had calmed down a bit now and could see the logic in what I was trying to say.

'See, Shubhangi, how can I tell you what you should do? Our lives are all about the decisions that we make. Getting married to this guy was a decision you made years ago. Don't get me wrong, but to let him behave towards you like an animal was also a decision. If you had stopped him the very first time, do you think he would have dared to treat you like this? People always treat us the way we allow them to. If you choose to become a punching bag, you will keep getting punched all your life. Today it's your husband, tomorrow it will be someone else. You have to decide for yourself what would you want to be – a punching bag or a strong woman who believes in herself.'

'I am now starting to realize my mistake, Rinku. I alone am responsible for all the mess in my life. I chose to become a punching bag and forgot who I really was. What am I teaching my girls? To let men treat you whatever way they like? My God! What a huge mistake I have made! How did I forget myself?'

I could see a spark coming back in her eyes. I knew this realization was enough to make the change happen in her life.

'Promise me one thing, Shubh, you will take back your power and create a life that you want and deserve. I am always there for you.' We then hugged each other and parted.

A few months later, I got a call from Shubhangi, informing me that she had moved out of her husband's house and had filed for a divorce. She would certainly have faced many challenges after this decision – the long and draining legal battle, the lack of finances, the unforgiving social scrutiny and what not – but she now had the clarity that on the other side of all these difficulties lay a good life, a belief that would give her strength and courage. Initially, she stayed at her parents' house and they helped her financially, while she applied for jobs. She had a bachelor's degree with a major in finance and marketing and she was exceptionally good at communications, so her efforts finally paid off and she got a job in a top consulting firm. She regained her confidence and slowly started building her life. Today, she lives in a spacious villa in one of the poshest localities in her city and is doing really well for herself. She is now divorced and coping happily with life. Her daughters too are turning out to be strong women like her. The same Shubhangi who thought that she and her daughters could not survive without the shield of a man is today a self-made success story.

Shubhangi's journey is a powerful one of how our decisions influence our life. Our decisions are what make or break us.

If you look closely at your decisions, you will realize that to a very large extent, our decisions are affected by our socio-economic status, age, likes and dislikes, beliefs and values, educational background and so on. Another important factor that controls almost all our decisions is our experiences. Good or bad, our experiences determine to a very large extent how we make decisions in our present.

Decisions are the *force* that determine the quality and direction of our life, as was in Shubhangi's case. The life that we are living is a direct reflection of our decisions. I want you to now take a moment and look back at your life five, ten, fifteen, twenty or more years back from today. Think of two or three major decisions (write them down if you want to) that you made then. It could be a decision related to your career, marriage, or business – anything of significance. Now ask yourself these two questions:

Would my life have taken a different direction (good or bad) had I made a different decision then?
Would the quality of my life have been different (good or bad) had I made a different decision then?

Your answers will illustrate the impact decisions have on your life.

Even small decisions can have a profound impact on our lives, when measured over the course of several years. Like the decision not to exercise or not to eat right. Over the course of several years, it will show its impact in the form of deteriorating health and we may find ourselves asking, 'How did I end up with a cardiac arrest?', not realizing that it happened because of the small but consistent decisions we made throughout in the past.

How do we define a decision? A decision is a commitment, a choice that you make based on how you feel, which is followed by an action. A commitment without action is not a decision.

Shalini, who is overweight, joined a gym. However, she found it hard to go to the gym every day. She felt lazy and was not driven enough to exercise on her own. This continued for years and she was losing her battle with her weight. One fine day, she 'decided' that she would go to the gym regularly, no matter what. The first day, she was very enthusiastic; the second day, her whole body ached but since she had 'decided', she didn't stop. The third day, she told herself in the morning, 'I need a break today. My body is tired. I will go tomorrow.' And that tomorrow never came. How many of us have been there? This happened because Shalini simply made a commitment to herself, while forgetting that consistent action is what would give her the desired results. It happens with most of us. We decide on something, we start with a lot of zeal and end up overworking ourselves, which leaves us exhausted and we eventually lose all our fuel and stop taking action.

The key is to take baby steps, small consistent actions, which will not overwhelm us and will help us get to the desired results. A simple equation for a decision is:

Decision = Commitment + Action

People often say that they find it hard to make decisions. In fact, over the years, I have found that most people find it very difficult to make decisions, so they tend to put them off. I have witnessed some senior leaders in Fortune-500 companies who are afraid of making the wrong decision. That's probably because they associate more pain with making the decision than with *not* making the decision. This is what I call 'decision paralysis.' Unfortunately, there is no way we can avoid making decisions. We all have to make decisions all the time, ranging from trivial ones, like what to have for lunch, right up to life-changing decisions, like where and what to study or whom to marry and so on.

Decision paralysis stems from Mr Saboteur whispering doubts about your decision in your ears, so it feels more comfortable simply not making the decision or putting it off for as long as possible. However, the problem with this line of thinking is that we do not consider the cost of this behaviour. This might lead to our missing out on so many opportunities because we chose not to act. Opportunities knock at our door once and if we choose not to grab them, they will go knock at someone else's door. Therefore, the timing of the decision is also immensely crucial. We cannot keep waiting endlessly to make a decision about, say, what subjects to graduate in, can we?

The major factor that causes decision paralysis is *uncertainty about the consequences* attached with decisions: *Will the outcome be what I anticipate?* Decisions are difficult because we try to predict the future. If we had all the facts and could accurately predict the future, decision making would have been a cakewalk. This, of course, is not possible. Though gathering the relevant information and facts is possible, the unpredictability attached with decisions still makes them difficult. We put them off because we have a belief that a decision shouldn't be made until we are certain that it is right. The truth is that decisions are always made based on probability and not certainty. For example, when hiring a new employee, you do a series of interviews, conduct background checks, get the relevant referrals and eventually you must decide, either to hire him/her or not. You cannot postpone it indefinitely until you are sure about the candidate, because that certainty will never come. Don't wait for absolute certainty, because you will almost never get it. This does not mean that we go and make reckless decisions. Weigh your pros and cons, get as much information as possible and then decide.

Some people allow others to make decisions for them due to the fear of them being wrong or the fear of the outcome. They don't want to *take responsibility* for the result of their decisions. I have seen many people, especially homemakers, who have given away their power to their spouses to decide for them. From the outside, this looks like compliance, but the underlying subconscious reason for this behaviour is that they are not ready to take responsibility if in case the decision is wrong. They tend to shy away from making decisions because they are not ready to own their failures. This attitude can prove extremely detrimental in the long run.

Another very interesting aspect is that decision-making is not just logical but also emotional. Following are the latest neuroscience findings.

Antonio Damasio, a neuroscientist, made a ground-breaking discovery a few years ago. He studied people who had damaged the part of their brain where emotions are generated. He found that these people were perfectly normal, except they were unable to feel many emotions.[1] Another common factor amongst them was that they couldn't make decisions. Logically, they could describe what they should be doing, but they found it difficult to make even simple decisions, such as what to eat for lunch. There is no rational way to decide what to eat – a pizza or a burger – so these test subjects were unable to arrive at a decision.

When it comes to decisions, emotions are thus very important. Even what we believe to be logical decisions are, in fact, always based on emotions. If you go back to the list of decisions you have earlier made, you will realize that all these decisions were essentially based on emotions. Even in Shubhangi's case, it was her emotions that kept her in her bad marriage for fourteen years. She believed that staying in the marriage would keep her and her daughters safe; it was the need for a sense of security (which is an emotion). It was the fear (another emotion) of the unknown – of what would happen if she were to walk out.

When you decided on a career path, you wanted to achieve something that would make you *feel* secure. We often hear couples say 'It just FELT right!' when asked how they decided to get married. You decide to eat a pizza over a burger, because the way a pizza makes you FEEL is different from the feeling you experience when you have a burger and maybe you like the former better.

When it comes to making decisions, there is a simple tool that I use myself and encourage everyone to use as well. It once again employs the art of asking powerful questions before making an important decision. Here are the questions:

What is the outcome or result I want from making this decision?
If I achieve this outcome, how will I feel?
Why do I want to achieve this outcome? How will it change my life for the better?

This will bring a lot of clarity and you will know if the decision will help you move forward or keep you stuck where you are. These questions will also help you get in touch with the emotions you want to experience, which is very important, because emotions are key to making decisions.

The organ in our body where all our emotions reside is our heart. The HeartMath Institute in California, which has been conducting extensive research on the human heart since 1991, has found that our heart has intuitive intelligence.[2]

So, whenever you need to make an important decision, ask yourself the above questions and listen to your heart: It never lies. You will get more clarity about your emotions and it becomes easier to decide. So don't ignore that small inner guiding voice. It's your best friend.

However, only emotion is not enough for making decisions. Whenever effective decision-making is required, there are a few more steps you need to follow:

- *Identify your goals (the three questions above will help you get clarity on this)*
- *Gather the facts and all the relevant information*
- *Analyze the situation*
- *Consider the alternatives*
- *Decide on a course of action*

Since decisions are based on probability and not certainty, there is always a possibility of your decision going wrong or not giving you the result you envisioned. This is when good decision-makers modify their original decision and continue moving forward. The more decisions you make, the better you will get at them. So don't hesitate to make decisions. Follow your heart, gather the facts, analyze the situation, consider alternatives and then take ACTION – consistent action. If you are not getting the desired results, modify your decision and continue the cycle again. Making a decision and acting on it is always better than not acting at all. You will become a proficient decision-maker when you keep making decisions and not repeating the mistakes that you made in the process before.

Sometimes, you don't have to make the decision yourself but instead influence other people to make a decision that you want. The one big factor that makes this possible is, again, emotion. If you look around, you will find that we are flooded with countless advertisements on TV, the internet, print media, you name it. What are they trying to do? They are trying to sell. What is their strategy? They are simply playing with your emotions. If an advertisement makes me feel a certain way, which I like, I will in all probability end up buying the product.

Emotions are at the root of all your personal, social, professional, and daily decisions. This revelation has helped me greatly with my work, especially with corporate people. I remember one such client, Nitin, who was new in the corporate world and was handling negotiations. During our conversations, I realized that he depended mainly on presenting facts, logic, and reasoning to hammer out a deal. However, he was finding it difficult to crack these deals. He said, 'Rinku, so often, after presenting an argument with bulletproof facts, reason and logic, we believe that there is no way the other party can say "no" to our proposal. But we find them still refusing our proposal. This is something that leaves me shocked. I don't understand the reason behind this behaviour. We feel like we have made an irrefutable case, but the other party fails to say "yes". This is causing me a lot of anxiety.'

'When you present your case to the other party, can you by any chance make sure that they see things your way?' I asked him.

'I guess not, because there is no way I can do that,' he answered.

'That's because you overlook the real factor that drives the other party's decision. See, you have to understand that behind any decision lies emotion. You have to help the other party discover for themselves what feels right and most advantageous to them. Their final decision will be based on only one thought: "What's in it for me? Is this good for me?" That is an emotion. So, the key is to present your pitch in a way that helps create a desirable vision in the other party,' I explained.

'That sounds really interesting. Could you explain a bit more?' Nitin was now smiling.

'I have already given you the key. But let me share a simple guideline with you. Start the conversation by building a good rapport with them. Rapport means simply making them feel important and comfortable by your gestures and words. Once a good rapport is established, share a previous success story with them. This will help build trust. Then ask them questions to get them to share their concerns, problems, unmet objectives and pains. This shows that you care. Then, you start building a vision for them, showing how your solutions are the best for all their problems. This vision should be the most desirable one for the other party.'

'Wow, this sounds like the ultimate solution,' he exclaimed.

'Nitin, I don't know if you noticed, but everything I shared with you is based on how you are making them feel. If you can leave them with a feeling, "This person really understands our concerns and he seems genuine," then 90 per cent of the battle is won. The remaining 10 per cent, your facts and reasoning will manage.'

In the next seven days, Nitin prepared an excellent generic pitch that he could easily customize based on his clients. What I explained, at the end of the day, was that we are dealing with humans and all humans are 'beings of emotions'. If you can touch their hearts and souls and make them feel the way they want to feel, you can influence their decisions. Today, Nitin is one of the top negotiators in his organization.

So, go all out there. Make your own decisions fearlessly. Remember you are the master designer of your life. It's your life and your decisions; you and only you are responsible for your life.

> ***'When someone makes a decision, he is really diving into a strong current that will carry him to places he had never dreamed of when he first made the decision.'***
>
> ***– Paulo Coelho***

When we make a decision, it can either lead to success or to failure. So, what happens if we fail? This brings us to our next idea.

3

FAILURE IS YOUR HIGHWAY TO SUCCESS

Do you have dreams or goals that you are hesitant to pursue?

Have you ever missed out on an opportunity because you were afraid?

Do you often base your decisions on the amount of fear that you feel?

Think about these questions and write down whatever comes to your mind. What dreams you have given up on? What fears have stopped you?

Around 90 per cent of people will answer 'Yes' to the above questions. What is stopping people from pursuing their dreams and making them miss out on great opportunities? There could be many reasons, lack of time, finances, facilities, skill, knowledge and so on. But these are not the only factors that stop us. The biggest factor, in fact, is our own fear. We are afraid of new experiences, disappointments, failures, maybe also to make a fool of ourselves. This fear robs us from our dreams. Fear is yet another deadly weapon of the Secret Saboteur. Fear is the thief that leads to passivity, and passivity creates doubt and uncertainty.

Fear is an insidious obstacle and, unfortunately, one that can hold you back. Nature created fear to help us survive in the stone-age when we lived in caves, when large predatory animals posed a threat to our survival. A keen awareness triggered by fear would save the lives. Once the threat was gone, the fear would dissipate.

Now, however, there just aren't as many real threats to our survival. Inside our brain, however, we still have the same fear circuit that our cave-dwelling ancestors did, but instead of acting up when a tiger is close, our fear circuit gets activated during modern day crucial situations, like public speaking, rejection, failure, disappointment, and heartbreak.

The trigger can be different for all of us, but the fear element is the same. Nowadays, almost all the fears that we experience are imagined fears; however, your mind doesn't know the difference between something that is real or if it is imagined. There are numerous types of fears that could be getting in the way of your achieving your biggest goals and dreams. However, all these conscious or unconscious fears are born out of two fundamental fears: the *fear of failure* and the *fear of rejection.* Fear of rejection has been dealt with in detail in the next chapter. In this chapter, I talk about the *fear of failure.*

Vinita came to me for counselling because she felt imperfect. She was happily married and had two lovely daughters. She had a stable government job in the Indian Railways and she and her husband were financially sound. She said that she felt guilty about not feeling happier, because she was aware that she has had a good life. During my coaching sessions with her, I found out that she had always wanted to be a dancer. During her high school days, she had auditioned for a dance competition in school but had been disqualified. This left her heartbroken, and she started believing that maybe she was not 'a good enough' dancer and that she didn't have it in her. Her first failure made her believe that she wasn't good enough. Upon further probing, I realized that she feared failing again, so she never tried again. We discovered an obvious pattern in Vinita's life: giving up on anything she failed in the first attempt, whether it was her battle against her weight or learning a new skill such as driving. The list went on and she started discovering how her beliefs about failure had influenced her life.

Vinita is not alone. Many of us give up after failing at something. We are so disheartened that we start believing things that are not true, such as 'Maybe it was not meant for me' or 'I am not smart enough' or 'I don't have it in me'. Fear of failure lies at the heart of our unwillingness to try something again after we've failed at it. In most cases, we allow failure to define who we are. For Vinita, it meant giving up her dancing. For a budding new entrepreneur, a failure might seem to mean he/she was never destined to do business. A writer who fails to get their first book published might start to believing that they are not meant to be a writer.

We become what we choose to believe about ourselves after a failure. If we choose to give up each time we fail, the idea that failure is acceptable gets reinforced. This prevents us from trying again, leading us to miss out on many opportunities in life.

People who are afraid of failure are essentially afraid of making mistakes. We've been taught all our lives to avoid making mistakes and to instead strive for perfection. However, nobody on this planet can ever be perfect. We are all imperfect and our imperfections make us human. Making mistakes and failing are absolutely alright as long as we learn from them and grow and do not commit the same mistakes over and over again.

J. K. Rowling is one of the most famous failures, and it's a badge she wears proudly. Although she is now a self-made billionaire, she strongly believes that her many failures shaped her into the woman she is today. She admits that, at one point, she had failed immensely in her life. She was in a broken marriage, poor, and unemployed. And although she eventually found massive success with the *Harry Potter* series, the manuscript was rejected twelve times before eventually getting published.[1]

We tend to give up on our goals after we experience a failure only if we have developed some inaccurate or unproductive beliefs about failure. How we perceive failure influences how we think, feel, and behave, as in Vinita's case.

Initially, when I suggested that she could learn dance again, she came up with a lot of excuses, 'I'm too old to learn or dance' and 'I'm not fit enough'. But once she could identify the beliefs she had about failure – beliefs that were preventing her from trying again – she started realizing that just because she failed once did not mean she would fail again. This new belief made her more open to the idea.

She started searching for dance schools and enrolled in one of the best dance schools. She started working on her fitness (something she had been struggling with for years); she suddenly found the motivation to alter her lifestyle and to get a fit and healthy body, which is a prerequisite for a dancer. I could see a tremendous change in her attitude, she was a lot happier, her language had changed, she looked younger, she was fitter, and she had become more optimistic towards life. One day, she called me to inform that she had decided to quit her government job to start her own dance academy. She had already prepared a business plan for her new venture. Her transformation left me astounded.

Whenever I meet her now, I am amazed to see a person who is so driven and motivated. She told me that even now there are many challenges in her life, because starting a new enterprise, especially for someone with no business experience, was not easy. However, she was open to failing and making mistakes. She realized that these mistakes and failures exist to teach us something new about our own capabilities, our strengths, our potentials, and things that we are not aware of.

She said she had learnt a great lesson from this experience and that she couldn't thank me enough. I told her to write her lesson down and sign it and give it to me as a memory. This is what she wrote:

> *If you have a big dream, you will face a lot of challenges and obstacles on the journey towards realizing your dream. The only thing that will keep you going is a 'never give up' attitude and to keep moving ahead. Don't hesitate to make mistakes, as they will show you what not to do. Be open to failures, as they show you what you can do better the next time. Create an action plan to accomplish your dreams; this will increase your chances of success. On this beautiful journey, sometimes you might have to work on improving your skills, at others, you might have to look for opportunities where your skills may be appreciated.*

Profound, isn't it? A lesson worth internalizing.

Failure helps build your character and personality by challenging you in new ways. It helps you identify areas in your life that are not working, areas that need your attention. It helps you discover your hidden strengths and potentials. A failure has the power to show you abilities in yourself that you've never before recognized. A journey full of failures is actually a journey of self-discovery.

In Vinita's case, simply changing her relationship with failure helped her regain her lost confidence. She no longer viewed failure as final but instead as an opportunity to evolve and grow. This new belief, this new relationship with failure, instilled in her an unbelievable confidence to handle future setbacks.

Learning how to persevere despite encountering failures increases your mental strength over time. You will recognize how failure can improve your performance. Understanding that you will be okay, even if you fail repeatedly, this self assurance offers great peace in life. Failures are truly blessings. They exist to ensure that with each failure you become better.

'Failure is part of the process of success. People who avoid failure also avoid success.'

– Robert T. Kiyosaki

4

ARE YOU A PEOPLE PLEASER?

Do you find it difficult to express a contrary view? Do you pretend to agree most of the time?

Do you end up apologizing all the time, even if you are right?

Do you find it hard to say 'No'?

Do you feel responsible for how other people feel?

If your answer is 'yes' to the above questions, then, welcome to the People Pleaser Club. People pleasing is the compulsion to please everyone, make others feel good, even if it's at your own cost. I have worked with many people who suffered from this syndrome. I call it the Looking Good Syndrome. Most of these people try to defend this behaviour, saying that there's nothing wrong in being a kind person. What's wrong with doing good deeds and being a good human? My only response to this is, 'Do you feel great when you do these deeds? If yes, then it's a sign of genuine kindness. However, if you feel miserable from within when trying to please others, then it's the Looking Good Syndrome.' This leaves most of them contemplative.

When your heart says 'No' but you keep saying 'Yes' on the outside, when you simply do not have the courage to say 'No', it is people pleasing and not kindness.

However, the question now is, why do people suffer from this syndrome? The problem is not the people pleasing behaviour; this behaviour is merely a symptom of a deeper issue. The root of this behaviour lies in our childhood conditioning and the environment we were born and brought up in.

For instance, imagine the case of a girl born in a traditional Indian patriarchal family where a girl's birth is not celebrated. The child faces rejection right from her birth. However, love is the basic emotional need of every human; when this basic need is not met, a person will try to find ways to satisfy this need. She will do anything and everything to get that love and approval of her family or loved ones, and the best way to get it is to try and please the people she wishes loved her. Somehow, unconsciously, she has decided that the only way to get love, acceptance, and appreciation is to comply and to try to please the people who mistreat her. Over time, people-pleasing becomes a way of life, a habit.

This habit is not restricted to a particular gender or situation, but the underlying cause is the same: a lack of self-worth rooted in childhood conditioning and environment.

When you don't feel worthy enough, you try and seek approval and validation to feel that worth externally. People pleasers hope that saying 'Yes' to everything will help them feel accepted, loved, and liked. Their biggest fear is the fear of rejection, which makes them do anything to avoid conflict and confrontation.

The fear of rejection is another deadly weapon wielded by the Secret Saboteur and is as dangerous as the fear of failure. These are the two biggest fears we possess.

This people pleasing behaviour has deep repercussions. I am reminded of Sameer, a participant in one of my long-term programmes. Sameer had been in the telecom industry for more than a decade but was unhappy with his growth in the company. He was a committed employee, but none of his hard work or sincerity had ever been recognized or rewarded.

I wanted to understand why he was not making any progress in his career. So I kept probing him to get to the root of the real issue. What I found about Sameer was that he was a quintessential people pleaser. On many occasions, he ended up doing other people's tasks, leaving him struggling to finish his own work. This ensued in him showing mediocre results.

Also, he was a conformist. Never, in all those ten years, had he ever expressed his views on any new project or assignment. He told me that on many occasions his personal opinion was contrary to the majority view, but he did not have the courage to interject or contradict. He always had lots of ideas, which he knew were unique and brilliant, but he did not have the courage to share them as he feared they would not be accepted or he might be ridiculed. So he kept them to himself. The fear of rejection, stemming from a lack of self-worth, had led him to retract into himself.

This people pleasing, and non-assertive behaviour led everyone in his work place take him for granted. No one ever asked him for his opinion. In fact, people perceived him as someone who was 'dumb' and did not have anything new to contribute.

Sameer initially blamed his seniors for being prejudiced and for not recognizing his efforts and his worth, but when I placed a mirror before him, he realized that it was him and not anyone else who was responsible for his misery.

People pleasing damages both your personal and professional relations. When I asked Sameer how his married life was, his answer was 'Not very great'. I was not surprised by his response, because the people pleasers' attempts to please others, affects their personal lives as well. Most of Sameer's family time was spent trying to meet the expectations of his extended family, be it his cousins, siblings, or friends. When I asked him what impact this had on his wife and children, he told me that sometimes it meant that he wasn't home in time for dinner or to put the kids to bed or spend quality time with his wife. This conversation made him realize that by constantly saying 'Yes' to his extended family, he was unavailable to his own family.

When he realized that his desire to be liked by everyone was seriously hurting him, Sameer decided to take charge and change this pattern. I suggested that the best way to change this pattern was to start practising to say 'No' when he really didn't want to say 'Yes'. Initially, it was difficult for him and it took some practice. To begin with, he was not sure how to say 'No'. He thought he needed an excuse, but he didn't want to lie. I encouraged him to not lie and simply say something like, 'I would have loved to, but right now, it's not possible for me,' without giving any long explanations.

When he started practising this exercise, he thought people would get annoyed with him, but he noticed that they didn't really seem to get offended. Suddenly, he had more time to spend with his family and more time for his office assignments. He could focus more on his work and deliver quality results. He could see the attitude of people, in his work place or personal life, start changing toward him. In no time, he felt worthier and could see how he was no longer hesitant to express his views without fearing rejection. He was extremely elated to find that most of his suggestions were well-received and appreciated. He had discovered a new side of himself, which he never knew existed.

If you don't have the courage to speak up and share your feelings, you can never form authentic relationships with people. Denying that you're angry, sad, embarrassed, or disappointed

– even when you're emotionally wounded – ensures that a relationship remains superficial. While it's important to impress your boss and show that you can be agreeable, being compliant all the time may be counterproductive, as in Sameer's case till he changed his behaviour. You'll never reach your greatest potential if you try to please everyone.

When your words and your behaviour are in harmony with your core values and true emotions, you can begin to enjoy a real life. When you stop worrying about pleasing everyone and instead are willing to be bold enough to live according to your own values, you will suddenly see your self-esteem soaring. You will have more time and energy to devote to your goals, you will establish healthier relationships and you will feel less stressed.

A profound thought for you: Don't be afraid of losing people. Be afraid of losing yourself by trying to please everyone around you. Losing sight of who you are and what your core values are is the worst thing you can do to yourself.

> ***'When you say "yes" to others, make sure you aren't saying "no" to yourself.'***
>
> ***– Paulo Coelho***

When you learn to cure the Looking Good Syndrome by saying 'No' when you really want to say 'No', you will start to feel the power within you. Believe me, your 'Yes' will have more value, if you learn the art of saying 'No'. When you are true to yourself and your feelings, people who are genuine will appreciate you and stick with you, no matter what. And that's what we want, isn't it?

5

READY FOR A CHANGE?

Why the fear of change will keep you from greatness?

In the previous chapter, I spoke about the root of all our fears: the fear of failure and fear of rejection. Stemming from these is another fear that disrupts our life and is another weapon of the Secret Saboteur. It is the fear of change. So, let me ask you first:

Do you fear change?

Most of us will answer in the affirmative. What needs to be understood first is why we fear change so much? Be it change in the context of an organization or change in our personal lives, we are all afraid of it. There is a popular saying, 'Change is the only constant in life', which is very true, but despite knowing this fact, we fear change all the same. Before we try to figure out why we fear change, let's examine what change actually means.

If we look around us, we will see that nature is constantly changing. Seasons change, all living beings, animals, and plants are born, mature and then die. Change is a universal, natural phenomenon, just like the law of gravitation. Can we avoid the physical changes that we experience with age? No. Then why are we so scared of change in other areas of our life? Change is inevitable. Resisting it is like resisting gravity, or any other natural phenomenon.

If we look at all the laws of nature, we will find that they exist to make our lives better. Imagine life without gravity. We would not be able to do anything at all!

Think about the things that mattered to you most when you were a child. Do the same things matter to you, in the same way, now? The toys and games you loved as a child – they no longer interest you. My point is that as we grow, we change, our priorities change, our likes and dislikes change, we evolve and mature. All this change is so natural and gradual that we don't realize how we eventually changed so much.

Most people fear change, be it small or big. I remember when I changed the seating arrangement of my team in my office for the first time; almost everyone was very uncomfortable. One of them came and requested me if we could go back to the old arrangement. I refused. I continued routinely switching the workstations of my team, so that they would learn to adapt to change. If they could adapt to small changes, then it would be easier for them to accommodate bigger changes in life, personal or professional. After a couple of months, I found my team members requesting me to change their workstations, as they realized that change helped their creative ability and also they felt positive about it. Even stagnant water rots; it needs to flow to remain drinkable. It's no different for us.

It's easy to say you want to change, but successfully making a change is hard. Being able to change means becoming a better version of yourself – emotionally, mentally, physically, and behaviourally. However, our habitual thoughts, emotions, and behaviours prevent us from implementing these changes, even when we know they will improve our lives.

The reason we shy away from change is that we try to *change too much quickly*, which leaves us overwhelmed, and we start associating change with a lot of pain. And whatever we associate with pain, we tend to avoid. New Year resolutions are the biggest example. The most common resolution is to lose weight and become fitter. You are so pumped up and motivated to live up to your resolution that you end up over-exercising and eating way less than your normal diet which leaves you worn-out, tired, and hungry. Now, that's a lot of pain. So you tend to give up within a couple of days or weeks.

A simple way of changing our attitude to change is to consider the cost of changing versus the cost of not changing.

A businessman, also my client, was at the top of his game for almost two decades, but then the IT revolution came and many new and younger players entered his field. He started losing business to them and within a year, he could see his revenues nose-diving. The financial crisis was so grave that he was unable to even provide medical cover to his employees. He was worried and stressed and ended up being depressed.

When I spoke to him, I realized that he was not using new technology in any department of his organization. Everything was being done in the old conventional way – sales, marketing, production, you name it. I told him that it was the age of technology and he would have to keep up. Initially, he was reluctant to accept the fact that the times have changed and that he should adopt to the new ways of doing business. He said it would cost him a lot to revamp his systems, plus he would have to upgrade his and his team's skills in technology, which he thought was too much of a hassle.

I gave him a simple exercise. I asked him to write down all the consequences of revamping the system, good or bad. On another page, I asked him write down all the consequences of not changing anything. Then he would have to compare the two and share his thoughts with me. The next day, he came up to me, smiling and excited, and showed me the exercise. As predicted, the number of positives of revamping his system was much higher than of not changing. I asked him if he understood my point and these were his words:

'Rinku, when I did this exercise and sat with both the sheets and compared the results, I realized my fear of change, which was more a fear of the unknown, was so unwarranted. I realized that if I don't change with the changing world and keep up with the new technologies, my company would shut down in no time, which is way more painful. The only chance of survival is to upgrade myself and my teams and my systems.'

This realization helped him get back on track and today he is back in business, doing even better.

I have worked with so many people who are stuck in low-paying jobs that don't challenge or excite them, yet they are not willing to change their jobs. Despite feeling incredible stress about their financial situation and the lack of creativity in their current jobs, they are afraid to apply for new jobs. They are worried that they might not like a different job, they lack confidence in their skills, and they dread the thought of getting used to a new office, a new boss and different co-workers. This is when the above exercise helps them see the cost of their reluctance to change. I highly recommend this exercise if you are stuck with an important decision. It is simple, yet very powerful.

Another important technique that you can use to be open to change is to be on the alert for any negative self-talk or language you use on a day-to-day basis. Some of the negative thoughts and language that would tempt you to shy away from change are:

It will be too stressful to give up the things that I like.
What I am doing now isn't that bad.
There's no point trying, because I tried something like that before and it didn't work.

I don't handle change well.

I can't imagine myself surrounded by new people.

Be aware of these conversations and preferably write them down as soon as you catch yourself talking like that. Then, simply flip whatever you have written down and write down a contrary statement or a powerful question, even if you don't believe in it. For example, let's take the statement '*I can't imagine myself surrounded by new people*'; flip it and instead write, '*What if I end up meeting better people?*' Now that you have asked yourself a 'solution-based question', your brain will start thinking in that direction and might come up with answers like: If I end up meeting better people, it will be an opportunity for me to learn more and become better, or maybe I will find good friends among them. You never know what answers your brain will produce, but it will certainly be an empowering one.

In my personal experience, I have seen that often when people become committed to creating a change in one area of their lives, such as creating a debt-free life, before they know it, they are also losing weight, becoming physically fitter and their relationships start improving. Adapting to change in one area can also have a cascading effect in all the other areas of your life.

The truth is that all change is good. It causes us to grow and evolve and introduces us to who we truly are, what we are capable of. Change causes us to shift the way we view the world. Change, when embraced, can move us out of complacency into the higher reaches of our best self. Change can help us view opportunities that were previously dormant. Even the most painful changes, like divorce, accidents, illness or death, offer us powerful lessons. Life is unpredictable. Sometimes it brings us joy, success, fulfilment and sometimes everything seems to go awry, ranging from financial worries, health issues or failing relationships. These are situations we have no control over, but we always have control over how we respond to them.

Braving all these challenges will make you stronger, wiser, and better. We all have the habit of resisting change – but when things are not to our liking, we wish for change. When it is summer, we wish for winter; when it is winter, we wish for summer. When things are difficult, we wish they were easy. Let's wish that we become greater and bigger than all the difficulties and challenges life throws at us.

> ***'Don't wish it were easier, wish you were better. Don't wish for fewer problems, wish for more skills. Don't wish for less challenges, wish for more wisdom.'***
>
> ***– Jim Rohn***

Now that we know how to ask ourselves the right questions, make and own our decisions, handle and learn from our failures and be open to change, we are ready to take more risks.

If not, let's see how and why it is necessary to take risks in order to win the big prizes in life.

6

INVESTING IN TAKING RISKS IN LIFE

Are you scared to jump into the unknown?

How often do you refuse to take risks that might cause you discomfort?

How often do you spend time daydreaming about what you love to do, without taking any action in that direction?

How often have you thought about taking a risk, but ended up being cold feet, because every time you think of taking a risk, you end up imagining the worst-case scenario?

Do you believe that all the outcomes in life depend on luck?

If you have responded in the affirmative to the above questions, then you are scared of taking risks. This fear of taking risks is also the work of the Secret Saboteur.

The world is full of uncertainty. Life itself is uncertain. None of us knows what the next moment holds for us. We still want to stick to life patterns that seem to be in our control. The truth is, nothing is in our control. We are all living in a sea of uncertainty.

It is this clash between our *wanting* to plan and decide our lives on certainties and yet being aware that everything is uncertain that makes us afraid. We want to stay with what seems more certain rather than risk trying something that seems less certain. We know there is uncertainty, and we fear it. We try to pretend we can ward it off by staying stuck in a 'safe' place. We want more but are afraid of the risks involved with trying to attain it. We spend time worrying about our future, trying to make every step secure, when the truth is that no one knows what the future holds.

If we look at the business world, in the past fifty years, it has seen the rise and fall of numerous Fortune-500 companies and the birth of new industries, which further proves that uncertainty is an inevitable part of our lives.

We face risks in almost all areas of our life, be it financial, physical, emotional or social, yet most of us are averse to taking risks. We think we are safe in our current jobs or careers, but where is the guarantee that we will stay there forever? This goes for our relationships too – where is the guarantee that they will stay the way they are right now? Again, where is the guarantee that we will continue to enjoy good health forever? There is risk all around us. Even if we take no risks, our lives will still be fraught with risk. The decision to not take risk too holds some amount of risk!

The primary reason for this aversion to taking risks, is fear. Fear is a paralyzing emotion. It makes us focus more on the 'what if(s)' rather than on the 'what could be(s)'. We often avoid taking risks that could help us reach our full potential.

When I talk about taking risks, I don't mean taking reckless risks; I mean taking calculated risks. But how many of us know how to calculate risks? This lack of knowledge about how to calculate risks causes more fear. And when there is more fear, it ends with further avoidance of risks. Calculating risks is not very difficult; it is like any other skill, and you can learn it. Once you learn this skill, your ability to take calculated risks will improve. I have devised a risk-calculating system, which I call the 'Six Magic Steps', to help one calculate risks and make prudent and well-informed decisions.

- **Step One:** Write down all the possible outcomes of everything going as desired. Next, write the impact (emotional, physical, financial, social) these positive consequences will have on you. Will your finances improve? Would it improve your relationships? Would it lead to improved health (emotional and physical)?
- **Step Two:** Write down all the outcomes that will occur in the worst-case scenario. Then write the impact (emotional, physical, financial, social) these negative outcomes will have on you. How will you respond if this scenario did occur? What steps could you possibly take to increase your chances of success?

- **Step Three:** Do more research and gain as much information as possible if you feel you don't know enough. However, if more information is not available, make the decision with whatever information you do have.
- **Step Four:** Have a clear vision about what you really want in your life. Write it down. Then examine and write how this risk would play a role in achieving this life goal.
- **Step Five:** On a sheet of paper, make two columns. One column is for benefits and the other for costs. You already have them written in the first four steps. This step will help you compile it all on one page.
- **Step Six:** Finally, listen to your intuition; your heart. It never lies and it already knows what is best for you. Keep the sheet of paper with the benefits and the costs in front of you and see if the payoffs outweigh the costs. Then close your eyes and ask yourself, 'How would this decision change my life?'

Let me explain this with an example. Imagine you want to purchase a new house and you don't have all the finances at present, but the deal that you are getting right now is profitable and is being offered for a limited time. This house fulfils all the parameters of your dream home, and you don't want to let go of this opportunity, but then there are risks – the biggest one being the financial risk. How will you arrange the finances? Also, there is another risk related to the time of delivery of the house. What if the builder does not deliver the house in time?

You should now calculate the risks, based on the steps mentioned above. Let's consider the first scenario, when everything goes as per the plan, the outcomes are all desirable. The consequences of the outcomes could be: Living a good life with all the facilities and amenities that you have dreamt of, leading to more happiness in the family, so on and so forth.

Now take the second scenario, which is the worst-case scenario. The outcomes could be: You face financial challenges, the house is not delivered on time and you end up living in a rented accommodation forever.

Now, what is the probability of the latter coming true? For that, you would need to research on the past history of the builder, which would give you an idea about his work. Next, you can plan your finances, sitting with a financial expert, and figure out the feasibility of the risk. Based on all this information, you would be in an apt position to take a prudent decision.

Then follow the remaining three steps. This exercise will then give you the courage to take that risk and go after your dreams.

Deepak, a participant in my workshop, was in a corporate job but always dreamt of owning his own business. Though he was at a high position in his career, he never felt fulfilled because his heart was not in his current job. He had some brilliant ideas as well. However, his biggest challenge was financial insecurity. In the past, he had made some bad investments due to which he had incurred massive financial losses. Whenever he pictured himself starting a business, he was reminded of those past experiences. So his thoughts about taking another *big* risk were immediately negative. He imagined himself going bankrupt, becoming homeless and penniless and dependent on others in his old age. Whenever he thought about his business, he would feel like he had jumped off a plane without a parachute.

This exaggerated negative thinking caused more fear and anxiety and prevented him from taking any action. I told him to do the Six Magic Steps and share his thoughts with me after. When he shared the results with me, I was surprised to see not one or two but twenty sheets of paper!

He had done this exercise in detail and he said something that I still remember: 'I calculated my risks like this for the very first time. The one thing that I realized after doing this was that I had never calculated the emotional toll that avoiding this risk was having on me. Not following my dream had affected my happiness for so many years of my life. I realized I had wasted all those years just because of my unfounded fears.'

Today, Deepak is the proud owner of a thriving business. Whenever he meets me, he tells me that he wonders why he hadn't taken this step earlier. He is doing so well because now he is doing what he loves and has overcome his biggest fears. That's the power of taking calculated risks. Often we incorrectly assume there's a direct relation between the level of our fear and the level of risk, but if we calculate the risk using the Six Magic Steps, we will know which risks are worth taking and we will be a lot less fearful about taking them.

Richard Branson, founder of the Virgin Group, is a known risk-taker. This attitude took him from being a dyslexic kid who struggled academically to being the owner of various music companies, airlines and mobile phone companies. Today, his estimated net worth is $ 500 millions. However, Branson agrees that all his risks are calculated and, in his words, they are 'strategic judgements, not blind gambles'.[1]

Remember, the future belongs to the risk-takers, not the security-seekers. Life is strange, in the sense that the more you seek security, the less of it you have. But the more you seek opportunity, the more likely it is that you will attain the security that you desire.

> ***'The biggest risk is not taking any risk. In a world that's changing really quickly, the only strategy that is guaranteed to fail is not taking any risks.'***
>
> ***– Mark Zuckerberg***

When we take risks and charter new territories, we need something that will keep us going, regardless of the hurdles and challenges that we might encounter on this journey. The next part of the book 'Take Charge' shows us exactly how to do this.

II

TAKE CHARGE

7

CLARITY OF VISION

Why clarity of vision is crucial to achieve your goals?

Are you happy with who you are?
Are you happy with where you are in life?
Are you happy with what you have achieved and where you are going?

If you have honestly answered the above questions, then you know where you exactly stand in your life. Very often, we feel like we are living lives that someone else wanted us to live – our parents, our near and dear ones or even the society we are a part of. Our life is a journey and like any journey, this journey will be fruitful only if we know what our destination is and the direction in which we are going. Without a clearly defined destination and direction, we end up in a career we do not feel great about or in relationships that don't work out which have a bad effect on our health. All this happens because we do not have clarity on what it is that we are trying to accomplish.

One emotion and state of mind that many people find quite difficult to deal with is the sense of not having any clarity or a state of confusion. We feel powerless, clueless, and frustrated when we don't know what we want, why things are as they are, what to do, or which way to go. This state of confusion is yet another destructive weapon of the Secret Saboteur, which leaves us befuddled and directionless, with a feeling of not being in control of our own lives.

So, it is worth spending time trying to figure out what exactly we are trying to accomplish. Otherwise we will find ourselves asking, 'How did I end up here?'

For gaining this clarity, it is important to know some things: What is it that you really want? What do you want professionally, personally, for your family? What is your vision for your life? You also need to know *why* you want what you want. Knowing the why is important, because this is what will keep you enthusiastic and focused all your life.

Clarity is all about knowing the answers to the 'what(s)' and 'why(s)' of your life. You already know that you need to frame your questions well. Here, I talk about the motivations behind them and, by extension, the direction in which your motivation takes you.

So much has been written about the ingredients for success. Some say you need perseverance, determination, passion, knowledge, action, to succeed. They are all indeed important to create success. However, the one most essential ingredient is *commitment*. But commitment comes only with *clarity*. You need to know what to commit to and why. The 'what' gives you the goal – what you want to accomplish, your destination – and the 'why' gives you the direction – why you want to accomplish it. This kind of clarity is extremely potent. It gives you confidence, a sense of purpose, peace and fulfilment. Instead of wasting two or three decades before realizing that you're not doing what you were meant for, if you start with clarity, it saves you time, heartache and so much more.

When I say clarity, it refers to clarity in all areas of your life, be it health, finance, career, relationships or business. You need to clearly know the 'what' and 'why' in these areas.

Clarity is the foundation on which we can build our dreams. Success lies in clarity. Just like all successful organizations have a clearly defined vision, mission, and goals, every single one of us too needs such clarity in our lives. When we start to ask ourselves with sincerity what we truly want, clarity will come.

◈

Rajeev, a young software professional at a renowned company, was a participant at one of my workshops. He told me that he chose to join my programme because he always felt that there was something missing in his life. Though he was doing well in his career and financially, he still did not feel great about his life. He said he did not feel alive from deep within. A twenty-something telling me that he didn't feel alive was a serious issue.

When I probed him, asking him the 'what' and 'why' questions, he was clueless. He said he never thought like that.

That's when I realized that he needed more clarity in his life. So, I ran past some questions and asked him to sit down and write the answers to them all. It would help him shift his focus to the real essence of what he really wanted.

I asked him what it was about his life that bothered him the most. He said that, more than anything, he did not like his work, but he did not know what else to do if not software programming. It was the only thing he was sure about.

I asked him if there was anything else that interested him that he liked doing or exploring, something he enjoyed talking about and for which people came to him for advice. Initially, he could not figure out anything significant. I told him to take his time and ponder on this for a couple of days. On the last day of the programme, he came up to me and said that he had always been intrigued by organic farming and, as a hobby, would research extensively on the different techniques used for organic farming. He had immense knowledge about the different types of organic foods and how they helped maintain proper health. He also told me that most of his conversations with his friends and family, revolved around this.

I could see how passionate he was about organic farming, as he continued talking about organic farming and how beneficial it is, not only for our health but also for the natural resources and the environment. He told me that organic farming is a system that favours the use of organic materials and microbial fertilizers to improve soil health and increase yield, which would in turn change the face of agriculture of our country and help in facilitating economic development. I was so impressed by his passion and knowledge of the subject that I wondered what he was doing in a software company.

I then asked him what was stopping him from pursuing his passion. If he was so passionate and knowledgeable about organic farming, why was he not pursuing it? And the answer was, as in most cases, '*What if* it doesn't work? I don't have the finances.' I left him with the following question: 'If you knew there was absolutely no way you could fail and if time and money were not an issue, would you then pursue it? And how would you feel if this dream did come true?'

A year and a half later, when I had completely forgotten about him, he called me up. I was wondering how he'd remembered me all of a sudden. He told me that after the programme, the question I had asked him had changed his life. It had given him clarity that organic farming was the answer to his 'what' and 'why'. This gave him the courage to pursue his dream with commitment and enthusiasm. Though he faced a lot of challenges in getting a land and other resources initially, but because he had now committed to his 'what' and 'why', he was fearless. Yes, clarity has the power to make you courageous and helps you follow your passion without fear. Rajeev told me how this decision had changed his life entirely. Because he was doing what he loved and doing very well now, it kept him in great spirits all the time and this happiness reflected on all the areas of his life; everything had improved manifold.

He said he had called to first thank me for showing him the way. Second, he wanted to know if there was any magic at play, because what he had accomplished in a year and a half was nothing less than a miracle. I told him that there actually was science behind it. Our brain loves clarity. The clearer we are about our intentions, actions, and goals, the easier it is for the brain to help us achieve it. If we are confused, the brain does not know what to focus on and think about. Without clarity, the brain is not focused, so we end up experiencing random events and people in our lives. However, when we are crystal clear about what we want and why we want it, our brain knows exactly what to think and focus on. As a result, we start experiencing the right opportunities and come across the right people – all of which help us accomplish our goals effectively. As the famous peak performance coach Tony Robbins rightly says, 'Where focus goes, energy flows.'[1]

Clarity will help keep your brain focused on what you want and a focused brain is the most powerful manifestation tool. In a more rational sense, when your mind is clear and focused, it identifies opportunities and interacts with people in a way that will further the vision and goal – almost without any conscious effort. It almost seems as though the universe is handing us these things miraculously! Things fall into place, because we make a proper place for them.

'Clarity is power – the more clear you are about exactly what it is you want, the more your brain knows how to get there.'

– Anonymous

If Rajeev can do it, so can you. That's the power of clarity. It ensures your endeavours are worthy of your time and energy. It's only a matter of choice. If you choose clarity over confusion, your life will be a true reflection of your dreams.

Most people I work with, ask me, 'How does one gain clarity?' Clarity begins with self-awareness and self-knowledge. In Rajeev's case, the first step I took was to help him discover what lay within him. He had it inside him all along but was not aware of it. I helped him gain that self-awareness. Everything lies within us; all we need is a guiding light to show us the way. I have added a few questions that can help you gain awareness and knowledge of yourself:

- *What is my intuition telling me to do that I am not doing right now?*
- *How do I feel about what I am doing right now in my life?*
- *What do I want more in my life? (Make a list.)*
- *What do I want less of in my life? (Make a list.)*
- *What is truly important to me?*
- *What do I really want in my life?*

Clarity is a tool that helps us overcome obstacles and reach new heights. Whenever you find yourself stuck in life, whenever you feel like you are confused about an important decision, ask yourself the 'what' and 'why' questions:

- *What is the outcome I want? (Your vision or goal)*
- *Why do I want it? (What your vision or goal will do for you)*

These are the two power questions that will guide you in the right direction. Clarity helps us make better decisions with ease. It helps reduce conflict and stress. It helps improve efficiency in whatever we do. Clarity of thoughts, intentions, and actions help you shape the life that you want.

> ***'Clarity is power. The more clear you are about what you want, the more likely you are to achieve it.'***
>
> ***– Billy Cox***

When we plant a new seed in the soil, how do we ensure that it grows into a healthy plant? We nurture it with the right manure and water it properly. Which means that we will get the desired results from all that we have learnt so far only when we nurture and take good care of all the components. Just like seeds need the right environment to flourish, so do all our lessons and wisdom. If the environment is conducive, only then will the seeds of wisdom flourish and lead to the results that we want. Let's now look at how we can create this environment.

8

CREATING THE RIGHT ENVIRONMENT

Is your environment hurting your chances of success?

Every new commitment that you make in your life, whether personal or professional, takes a little bit of your energy and time. Whether it is spending time with the kids, repairing the car, going to the gym, office work, or anything at all; it all takes some *time* and *energy*, the two most important and precious resources we have. These are precious because they are both limited.

So, how are you utilizing these resources? Are you utilizing them to grow and evolve as a person, or are you squandering them?

When you put your energy and time into something, be conscious of the outcome or result it is producing in your life. For example, if you catch yourself indulging in backbiting or gossiping, ask yourself, 'How is this serving me? Is this conversation making me a better person? Am I gaining anything of significance from this discussion?' If the answer is 'No', it means that you were wasting your time and energy in an activity that would eventually give you no positive outcome. Then why waste these precious resources?

We can create our best life if we learn to utilize our time and energy in the right manner and in the right things. One of the best ways to make this happen is to create an environment in and around us that is conducive to our growth, an environment where our time and energy is utilized in the best possible way. Now the question is, how do we create an environment like that?

Before getting into that, let's understand what I mean by environment.

Environment is anything and everything that we are surrounded by in our life. This could be our physical environment, which includes our house, car, office, clothes, belongings and so on. It could also be the people in our life – our family, friends, relatives, colleagues, neighbours, and community. All these things are external to us, so I call this our 'external environment'. Let's first look at how this external environment affects our lives.

To begin with, ask yourself, 'Is there anything or anyone in my external environment that/who is draining my energy?'

Write down whatever comes to your mind and keep this list with you. In all probability, this list will have names of some people in your life. The conversations, behaviour, and outlook of some people will be toxic for you. These people are 'Energy Vampires': they suck the life out of you. Whenever you are around such people you will end up feeling exhausted and mentally drained. Since you have limited energy, if you allow someone to take that away every day, you won't get it back. You will need to do something to recharge yourself, to get back to normal; if you don't recharge yourself after being with such people, you will end up with depression or anxiety without even knowing why.

Did you know that for every negative experience, it takes approximately thirteen positive experiences simply to bring you back to neutral? So, do you have someone in your life who makes you feel agitated? Do you have someone in your life who leaves you feeling disempowered and not good enough? Do you have someone in your life who makes you feel lesser and unworthy of success?

These are the 'Energy Vampires' in your life, people who are like parasites: they suck out your energy, happiness and sometimes even your tangible resources. Get away from them as soon as you can.

Radhika felt lethargic and complained of lack of energy all the time. Even if she had had a good night's sleep, she would wake up feeling tired. She wondered if it had anything to do with her health, so she got all her medical tests done. Fortunately, everything was fine and according to the reports and her doctor, she was perfectly healthy. He gave her some supplements when she continued complaining of fatigue. But even they did not make her feel any better.

She shared this with me when we met once. I told her to do the exercise described above and to make a list of all the people in whose company she did not feel good. She did the exercise and found that there were two people who always made her feel bad about herself. One was her work colleague, Savita, and the other was her aunt. It seemed that Savita always made her feel less competent at work by telling her that she was not made for the work she was doing; that Savita was way better than her, by finding faults in everything Radhika did. Radhika told me that she spent the greatest part of her day with Savita since they shared a workplace. Further, Radhika lived in a joint family with her parents and two uncles and their respective families. Radhika was actually doing quite well professionally and did not want to marry for at least another two or three years. This was one area over which her aunt harassed her everyday, causing her a lot of stress.

Me: There you go. These are the two people who are sucking the energy out of your life. Get rid of them and see your energy levels soar.

Radhika: How can I get rid of these people? I can distance myself from Savita, but what about my aunt? She lives in the same house.

Me: It's very simple, Radhika. You cannot control the presence of some people in your life. But you can choose how to respond to them. Whenever your aunt starts her negative chatter, change the topic or excuse yourself from that conversation. This is what I practise with the 'Energy Vampires' in my life, and it works. Initially, your aunt might feel annoyed, but eventually she will understand that you don't respond to such conversations, so she will stop it. You will need to practise this habit, and if you practise it enough, it will become second nature to you in no time.

Radhika was so fed up of her constant fatigue that she was ready to give this a try even though initially she was skeptical. In less than a month, she could feel her energy levels increasing and the annoying behaviour of her aunt and Savita changing. The two things that helped Radhika create this change in her life were:

- *Awareness* about the presence of 'Energy Vampires' in her life and the way they were affecting her
- Her *decision to safeguard herself from the negativities in her environment*. This, in some cases, could mean either eliminating negative people from your life by distancing yourself from them or changing your response towards them.

Remember, one of the most important decisions we make in life is around whom we choose to be. Your environment shapes who you are and who you will become. So, please don't surround yourself with individuals who do not add value to your life, people who want you to stay around to fulfil their needs but have no positive impact on you. Walk away from such conversations and relationships.

An obvious question here is what do you do with an 'Energy Vampire' who is a very close family member? Do what Radhika did. Whenever they start their disempowering conversations, either change the subject or if they are adamant about continuing their drivel, just excuse yourself from the conversation. Initially, they might feel offended, but eventually they will figure out that you don't encourage such conversations, so they will stop doing it, at least with you.

Choose to surround yourself with innovators, thinkers and great listeners, who aspire to create positive change and leave a mark and who are willing to help you create yours as well. If you look at the most successful people, you will notice that they always place themselves in environments full of like-minded people. Even such people have weaknesses that are no different from ours. Surrounding themselves with people who are on a similar journey allows them to learn more and become better. Successful people are extremely particular about who they spend time with. People with whom we choose to surround ourselves impact the way we think, feel, and act on a day-to-day basis.

American entrepreneur and motivational speaker Jim Rohn says, 'You are the average of the five people you spend the most time with.' People have a humongous impact on your life. So, just as you are cautious about what you eat or drink, be conscious about the people you choose to be close to.

Often we do end up becoming like the people we are around. 'Show me your friends and I will tell you who you are,' goes an old saying. You will eventually become the product of the people you surround yourself with. We are all reflections of the people we keep in our lives and interact with on a regular basis. So, it is imperative to surround yourself with the 'right people' if you want to realize your dreams and achieve your desired goals in life.

Now, how do you define 'right people'? These are people who make you happy, who make you laugh when you are low, and who help you in the best possible way when you are in need. These are people who genuinely care about you. They are the ones who are worth keeping in your life; everyone else is just passing through. The right people you are looking for are positive, happy people that enrich your life. They can be your family members, your friends, acquaintances, colleagues, or neighbours.

The right people are people who will inspire you to be a better person, motivate you to achieve your goals, encourage and empower you to make changes that are needed for you to be successful, and who will celebrate your success. These are the people who might not be like you, but they share the same core values as you. Having differing opinions and healthy arguments helps present new perspectives and gives an opportunity to grow your knowledge.

'Surround yourself with people who make you happy. People who make you laugh, who help you when you're in need.

People who genuinely care. They are the ones worth keeping in your life. Everyone else is just passing through.'

–Karl Marx

So, how do you identify these people in your life? For this, follow these steps:

- Begin your search in your existing networks and among the people closest to you. Make a list of these people. You can divide them into categories, such as friends, family, colleagues, co-workers, acquaintances and so on.
- Then, for each person, think about their qualities and ask yourself if they are a positive influence in your life. Ask yourself these questions:
    - o *Are they happy people?*
    - o *Do they encourage me to achieve my goals?*
    - o *Are they supportive when I need their support?*
    - o *Do they make me feel good about myself?*
    - o *Do I feel happy, inspired, and energized after spending time with them?*
    - o *Are these people genuinely happy to see my success and happiness?*

  If the answer is 'Yes' to all the above questions, then that person belongs to the 'right' category.
- Sometimes you want to be with people who are better than you in certain areas you want to improve in, but they might not be a part of your known circle. In that case, look around for experts and successful people who have already achieved

the goals you want to accomplish. These people can become a part of your environment through technology; watch their videos or read their books (if they have authored any).

People are different. Things that make me happy might not make you happy. Your idea of support might be different from mine. The key is to find people who are 'right' for you. This analysis will help you understand if the people in your environment add to your life or take away from it.

If you want to be financially successful, then surround yourself with people who are already financially successful. If you want to improve your relationship with your spouse, surround yourself with people in successful relationships. If you want to become successful, surround yourself with people who share your goals or who have already achieved some. A young entrepreneur is going to succeed if he surrounds himself with people who push him to better his abilities, people who themselves have walked or are walking the same path, not people who pull him down and discourage him. Want to start your own company? Start networking with established entrepreneurs who have already achieved what you want to achieve. If you are around someone with a cold, there is a good chance that you will catch the cold. Be very aware of what you are catching from the people around you.

Jack Ma, founder and CEO of Alibaba, says, 'I always hire people who I think are smarter than me.'[1] This is another trait of successful people. They choose to be surrounded by people who are better than them. This gives them an opportunity to learn and grow. Being the 'smartest' person in the room may be gratifying to the ego but is not conducive to growth. Richard Tirendi, CEO of VisionQuest, says, 'If you're the "smartest" one in the room, you are in the wrong room.'[2]

You are the sum of who you spend your time with. Make sure that you are directly involved with people who uplift, inspire, and motivate you to do and be more.

When I commenced my journey towards realizing my dream of impacting millions of people and creating a difference in their lives, I was not alone. I had people in my life who believed in my dreams and supported me unconditionally in accomplishing them. There were many challenges and I encountered umpteen failures; sometimes things would get so unbearable that I would feel like giving up. Those were the times when this environment of the 'right' supportive people came to my rescue and did not allow me to give up. I owe this success to all of them. I remember in the intial days, I could barely get clients and sometimes after all my efforts, no one would sign up for my workshops. This was a time when I was financially drained and emotionally a wreck and I wanted to give it all up. That is when my family, my husband and my son gave me pep talks and helped me believe in myself and my dream. Their constant support and belief in me helped me get back on track.

Besides the people in our life, we need to be careful of what we are absorbing from the different sources of information around us – they too are part of our external environment. We live in a world that is becoming increasingly digital by the minute. Almost everyone has access to smartphones and other devices that connect them to the internet 24/7. This digital world constantly tempts and distracts us, feeding us an unending stream of junk information. All the apps, services, and social media tap into our time and energy, draining it out over minutes and hours.

We get a lot of negativity regularly from media outlets, because that's what sells. Open the newspaper – it is flooded with negative news. Switch on the TV – there's plenty there as well. So, if you happen to be a 'news addict', you are feeding yourself negative images and information every day. Although these are realities of the current times that we can't ignore, we always have a choice. Choose what kind of information you want to feed into your mind, because whatever you feed your mind on a regular basis, your mind will create in your life. So, choose carefully and ask yourself:

> What information from the outside world, including the virtual/digital world, the TV or the print media, will enrich my mind and benefit me in the long run?

Then, make a choice!

Make rules that include developing habits to use technology and all the information available to nourish your mind, to grow and learn things that add value to your life. And then stick to these rules, no matter what.

I have a rule in my house. We don't watch news channels on TV, because they serve only negative news 24/7. Instead, we listen to the five-minute news on the radio at 10 a.m. every day to keep ourselves updated. You should decide what you want from these information channels that will help create the life you want; eliminate the rest. It's in your hands.

What else, other than toxic people and negative information, could be sucking your energy? Check the list you made at the beginning of this chapter. Is there something else there?

If it's a 'Yes', you know what I am talking about. I am talking about the things around us that we tolerate. These are things that bring us discomfort, but not enough discomfort for us to focus our attention on them and fix them. This is because you feel like you don't have the time or the energy to resolve them. These 'things' could be anything from clutter in your workplace or house or kitchen, a leaking water pipe, anything that you have been ignoring.

Let's borrow from science here and look at the very basic unit of existence, an atom. All living and non-living things are made up of atoms, which are 99.99999 per cent energy and are vibrating. Anything that is vibrating has a frequency. So, everything, including us, is vibrating energy and has a frequency. That means all the clutter too is vibrating and has a frequency, and when we are in cluttered environments, these mixed vibrations or frequencies drain our energy. Cluttered rooms influence our energy. Have you ever noticed how good it feels to stand in the foyer of a five-star hotel; we suddenly feel more energized. That's because there are no entangling frequencies there. Also, when we are in dirty surroundings, we feel gloomy. That's because cluttered and dirty environments have entangling energies, which counter our energy and drain us.

So, if there is clutter around you right now, whether you are in your office or home, just take ten minutes to clean it up. I guarantee you that you will feel a lot better after that. Cluttered environments not only sap your energy, they also clutter your mind and make you less clear-headed.

I am reminded of a client who had been running a business for more than a decade. He was doing moderately well but way below his expectations. He told me that he was not getting the volume of business that he expected despite being one of the best in his field. When I probed, I could not find anything that could be hindering his growth. Then I asked him if I could visit his office. What I saw there gave me the answer to his woes. His office, especially his cabin, was a mess. Everything from his files to his stationery was all over the place and there were layers of dust everywhere. I told him to do a simple exercise: to clean and organize everything in his cabin himself, at least for the next forty to fifty days. He looked surprised, but he respects me a lot and so he agreed.

After exactly two months, he called me and said that something magical was happening. He had started getting more business in the past month than he had ever gotten. He asked me how it was all happening. I told him about the significance of cleaning the clutter and organizing the world around us, so that it does not drain us. When our energy is positive, things automatically start falling in place.

This is the significance of this part of our environment that we often regard as not very important and hence often end up neglecting it. Cluttered environments drain your energy and then it's difficult to stay clear-headed and focus on your goals. Simply tidying up your environment – home, work place, neighbourhood – will help you focus more clearly on your goals. When you buy new stuff, make sure you get rid of the old stuff first. Don't just mindlessly keep hoarding stuff – be a minimalist. It will help you in your journey towards accomplishing your goals.

Let's now talk about the environment that we create inside ourselves: our 'internal environment'. The internal environment is the world of our thoughts and emotions, and the biochemistry of our physical body. The external environment has a profound impact on our internal environment. Our thoughts are directly impacted by what we feed our minds, whether it is the people around us or the digital medium, which we have already discussed.

According to neuroscience, the brain is a reflection of our external environment, our life. The people, conditions, and events that we've experienced and learned from are stored and organized in the neurological structure of our brain. I will not go into scientific details here. What I want you to understand is how these thoughts and emotions impact your biochemistry. Whenever we have a thought, it immediately produces chemicals in the brain called neurotransmitters, which act like messengers to the body. These transmitters enter the bloodstream and trigger a feeling that is in alignment with the thought. So, the moment we have a thought, we immediately start feeling how we think. That's because the transmitters from the brain trigger glands in the body to produce chemicals, which create a feeling in the body that is in sync with the thought.

So, if it is a fearful thought, the body will start secreting stress hormones and we will start feeling fear and anxiety. That's because the brain is in constant communication with the body and is always evaluating the internal chemical environment of the body. The body sends a message to the brain that it is now feeling the way the brain is thinking. This signals to the brain that it now needs to reinforce the same feeling in the body, so it makes more chemicals to strengthen the same feeling. This cycle continues until the brain chooses to change the thought. So, if we have a habit of ruminating on our fears and worries, the body will remain in the stress mode and the same stress chemicals will continue to flow through our bloodstream, which will eventually lead to disease and illness. Then we say, 'How did I end up with so many health issues? I exercise, I eat right. What went wrong?'

What went wrong is what you kept feeding your mind. If you keep feeding your mind toxins, it will keep creating more and more toxins in your body, which becomes the perfect breeding ground for diseases. In fact, the body's internal environment not only affects our well-being but also the well-being of the foetus inside a mother's womb. There is more in the mother's blood than just nutrition. Our blood has the chemicals of our dominant emotions. This chemical mix of emotions and all other factors that control the mother's body also enters the placenta and affects the foetus, both physically and emotionally. So, if the mother was stressed or anxious during her pregnancy, for example, there are greater chances that the baby will be born with stress and anxiety problems. If her dominant emotion was that of happiness and calm, then the baby would probably be a happy baby. The baby thus learns the patterns and behaviours of the mother even before it is born. This is the impact of a mother's internal environment on her unborn baby.

In an experiment conducted at the Primate Research Institute of Kyoto University in Japan, a pregnant mother chimp was being taught a computer programme. The mother had to turn on a computer and the Japanese script for colours would show up. On the bottom of the screen was a colour bar and if she selected the right colour to match the script, a coin would pop out of the computer. She could take the coin to a vending machine and buy a treat. It took many months to teach this programme to the mother.

She then had a little baby chimp called Ayumu. Soon after birth Ayumu had been always present while his mother performed this experiment. One day, the mother interacted with the computer programme and went to the vending machine, leaving him behind. Ayumu, who couldn't yet walk, pulled itself up to the computer and turned it on. The script and colour bar appeared on the screen, and he selected the right colour and grabbed the coin. Scientists doing this experiment were shocked. Who had taught the baby this programme, which the mother had taken months to learn? The infant learnt it by simply observing his mother, proving how our external environment can impact our behaviours and learning, starting right from our birth.

Earlier, I mentioned how everything, including us, is vibrating and anything that is vibrating has a frequency. Our most dominant thoughts and emotions determine our personal frequency. If our dominant thoughts and feelings are negative, then our personal frequency will be lower and if they are positive it will be higher. The universe too is nothing but an ocean of energy. We are all energy beings living in an ocean of energy. The universe has every possible reality in it in the form of vibrating energy, be it of good health, wealth, abundance, or a great life partner or of pain, poverty, stagnation, failures, illnesses, etc. Everything is available to us, good or bad. What gets attracted to us, however, depends on our 'personal frequency'. If our personal frequency is that of lack, pain, and fear, then all the possibilities with similar frequency will get attracted towards us in the form of people, events, or challenges. We will end up feeling perplexed over why we are encountering so many hurdles and problems one after the other.

The good news is that in the case of humans, it is possible to change our personal frequency, just by changing our dominant thoughts and feelings. We communicate with the universe with our personal frequency. We will attract from the universe things that resonate with our vibrational signature. So, become mindful of your dominant thoughts and feelings, because they control your life in more ways than you think.

Your internal and external environments shape you and your life. If you have BIG dreams and you want to make sure that you realize them, then it's important that you work towards creating an 'environment' that supports you and your dreams. Just as a seed will grow into a healthy tree when planted in the right soil and when in soil, its environment, nurtures it well. Likewise, when we live in an enriching and uplifting environment (internal and external), all our life's goals and dreams will become our reality in no time.

'We make the world we live in and shape our own environment.'
– Orison Swett Marden

9

BE A LIFELONG LEARNER

The stairway of success is made of steps of learning.

We are all born naturally curious. We want to learn. However, as we grow older, the demands of our personal and professional lives take away a big chunk of our time, leaving us unable to quench this natural curiosity. Our quest for knowledge seems to end after we don the tasselled hat and gown. We cease to be learners once the pressures of life start bogging us down.

Many people think that with their hectic lives and already brimming schedules, they should just focus on developing the skills they need to stick to their current jobs and be informed enough to survive and get by. This mindset is a definite path to mediocrity. Everyone wants to be successful, but the irony is that most people are not willing to put in the efforts required to create an extraordinary life.

One of the best and most effective ways to create an extraordinary life is to become a 'learner for life'. We all know our world is changing at a frantic pace and if we do not continue to evolve and grow at a similar pace, we will soon be left behind. To keep up with the ever-changing world, we all need to be lifelong learners. We need to continually polish our skills and keep up to date, so that we have an edge in everything we do. Though we all have a natural desire to learn, we do tend to give in to complacency. However, history is testimony to the fact that all the extraordinary and successful people were and are great learners. They are open to learning forever and are all learners for life, without an exception. They constantly strive to know more, learn and evolve, which enabled them to create a competitive edge that propels them to success in all the areas of life.

> ***'Live as if you were to die tomorrow. Learn as if you were to live forever.'***
>
> ***– Mahatma Gandhi***

Learning is an art that helps us expand our horizons; it's a skill that, like all other skills, can be developed. It is one of the key ingredients for success and helps create enriching and fulfilling lives.

Reading books is one of the best ways to expand your horizons, stretch your current frontiers, improve your knowledge and gain new insights and powerful thoughts. Indeed, books are our best companions. Most of the top successful people are voracious readers.

Warren Buffett spends five to six hours a day reading newspapers and about 500 pages of corporate reports.[1] Bill Gates reads fifty books a year. He says, 'Reading is still the main way that I both learn new things and test my understanding.'[2] Mark Zuckerberg reads at least one book every two weeks.[3] He reads about different subjects to learn more about different cultures, beliefs, histories, and technologies. Elon Musk grew up reading two books a day and taught himself engineering and rocket design.[4]

The first step towards becoming a lifelong learner is therefore to cultivate the habit of reading books. You could read books on subjects that interest you or anything else you fancy. I have always been fascinated with self-help books and biographies. One such book that changed the way I looked at my life and health was Louise Hay's *You Can Heal Your Life*. I was in my first job and for the first time realized that the quality of my life lay in my hands and that I could create good health myself without running to doctors and living on medicines. This book changed my life. Not only did I create good health for myself, I also gained clarity about what I really wanted to do with my life. This book was one of the many things that made me who I am today.

However, learning is not limited only to books. It could mean learning a new skill that interests you, such as learning a new language, a musical instrument or a sport. Studies have shown that whenever we learn something new, it helps us grow new brain cells and produce neurotransmitters, which help improve our long-term memory and reverse age-related decline in brain function.

Keeping our brains active and engaged in new areas also has cognitive benefits. According to the Global Council on Brain Health (GCBH), people who sew, knit, do carpentry or plumbing, play mind games or read have greater cognitive abilities as they age.[5] The GCBH recommendations also conclude that the more you engage your brain in cognitively stimulating activities, the lower your risk of Alzheimer's is.

Learning could even extend your life. A study published in the journal *Social Science and Medicine* concludes that those who regularly read books add years to their life.[6] In fact, in a long-term study of 3635 subjects, it was found that people who read for more than 3.5 hours a week lived two years longer than the non-readers.[7]

Thankfully, the pursuit of knowledge is a lot easier in the modern technological era. We have the privilege and convenience of accessing all information instantly, which makes learning even easier. We can listen to podcasts, watch videos, read blogs and so much more to gain knowledge. However, as I said in the previous chapter on environment, you should be aware of the kind of information you take in – negative, sensationalist, or junk material will do more harm than good. Also, avoid an information overload, as too much information taken in indiscriminately cannot be processed by our brain and does not convert to knowledge or learning. In fact, it can result in confusion.

Another important strategy is to learn from people who are more successful than us, irrespective of age, gender, caste, class, religion, or nationality. Look up to them and try and model their strategies. Do what they do, because they have already figured out what works, so simply model yourself based on them. This is a prudent way to create success in your life.

Although the above approaches are great to start becoming learners for life, there is one area that is often overlooked in the learning process, and I would like to dedicate this chapter to it. It is the ability and the humility to learn from all the people around us.

One of my childhood friends is a highly successful business owner today. She is someone who I find extremely inspiring. We had lost touch after school but happened to meet at a reunion. There I learnt that she has become one of the most successful women entrepreneurs today. I was extremely impressed by the fact that not only was she doing well professionally but her personal life too was great. We chatted for hours that day and she invited me to visit her office someday. I was so curious to see her at work that I decided to meet her again the following week.

I was at her stylish office, sitting in her luxurious cabin the following week when she had an urgent meeting to attend. She asked me to join too. One thing I noticed during the meeting was that she kept asking everyone for their opinions and everyone seemed more than willing to share their ideas, which was something one doesn't normally encounter. Most meetings start and end with the leader talking and the others taking notes. I could see that she was a highly receptive listener and genuinely cared about everyone's opinion. After the meeting, she took me out for lunch. I could not help asking her, 'Sakshi, do you always ask people for their opinions and ideas?'

She smiled and said, 'Yes, Rinku. For me, people are very important. Every single person in my company matters to me.'

'But why do you need to ask everyone for their opinion, when you yourself are so successful and experienced?' I asked.

Her smile became broader. 'That's because my success comes from some of the ideas of people I usually wouldn't be expected to ask. However, I have always been a learner and am open to learning from everyone and everything around me. I seek inspiration and learning from nature, plants, and animals too. There is just so much to learn from everything that sometimes I feel like a lifetime is not enough.

'I always see myself as a student of life. Rinku, you won't believe that some of my best business advice came from my mother's best friend who runs a small boutique. At times, it comes from our fresh recruits who we think don't have the experience. Once I was going through a financial crisis in my business and I shared it with my teenage son, because I wanted to vent, and he gave me some advice that was wise beyond his age. I followed his advice and got over that crisis in no time. That's when I realized the power of being open to learning from everyone and everything.'

This experience with my friend changed my entire perception of learning. She chose to be a student, even after she had 'made' it. There are people who think that once they have reached a certain 'level', they don't need to talk to people 'below' them, let alone ask for their opinion. A majority of people belong to this category. People who are educated and hold prestigious degrees believe that they are smarter than people who do not have such degrees or are uneducated. Some people have a belief that just because they have a grand title, an impressive degree, or more money, they can't learn from people who are not their 'equals'.

This prejudice happens not just in the workplace but also everywhere else. In society at large, we see people averse to seeking advice and opinions of people who belong to a lower social strata. Would you ever seek advice from or be open to asking the opinion of your househelp, your cook or your driver? Are you open to the idea that some of the best ideas or solutions for some of your current challenges might come from the most unexpected section of society? Sakshi is; and so am I. I learnt this lesson from her and it has served me really well.

I got great ideas for my articles and this book from people I thought did not know enough. I got extensive ideas about business strategies from people from different backgrounds, which proved helpful in scaling my business. I learn resilience, perseverance, patience, and a never-give-up attitude from my cook, who comes from a socially weak background and works really hard to make ends meet. Her husband is an alcoholic and has made life difficult for her, but she still chooses to remain happy and financially independent.

If you truly are willing to expand your mind, you need to rid yourself of the all the assumptions and prejudices, so that you are open and receptive to new information, regardless of the source.

Most people are not open because somewhere inside them they fear that asking people for advice will make them look 'bad'. This is nothing but the ego. Ego is the biggest enemy of learning. If you want to be a learner for life, stop making such assumptions and ask questions instead.

When we rid ourselves of all the assumptions and perceptions that we have formed about people over the years, it's like preparing the soil before planting anything new. We need to first get rid of all the weeds – the weeds of our preconceived notions.

At times you might also come across information that challenges and contradicts your worldview and beliefs. This is time to stop, introspect, and reflect on these new ideas in a way that can expand your vision and mind.

> *'Do you know the secret of the true scholar? In every man there is something wherein I may learn of him; and in that I am his pupil.'*
>
> *–Ralph Waldo Emerson*

Jack Ma is one of the richest men in China and the founder and CEO of Alibaba, one of the largest conglomerates of internet businesses. He is the first Chinese to be featured on the cover of *Forbes* magazine and was ranked second in

Fortune's 2017 list of the 'World's 50 Greatest Leaders'. He is a great example of learner for life. He says, 'Lessons about life and success are everywhere, but you must be willing to be open and learn.'[8]

Learning is a daily practice, which helps you explore new knowledge and ideas. Learning does not stop with school or college. The most effective and successful people are those who are learners for life, who are open to constant learning, regardless of the source, and compete against themselves to grow and evolve day by day.

Make a commitment to yourself today, to learn something new every day from your surroundings, be it from people, books, internet, nature or anything at all. You will be surprised to find that you end up discovering new concepts and ideas, which when applied will help you achieve the success you want. If you can cultivate this habit, it will make every day enjoyable and you will keep becoming a wiser and better version of yourself.

> ***'If you are not willing to learn, no one can help you. If you are willing to learn, no one can stop you.'***
>
> ***– Zig Ziglar***

The next chapter shares an idea that we often take for granted and do not realize the impact it has on our lives. If you can develop this quality, your life will never be the same again. So, what are we waiting for? Let's find out what it is!

10

THE POWER OF WORDS

Exercise the power of language to transform reality

We all know that humans are social animals who cannot live in seclusion. The most powerful way to socialize is through communication. One of our greatest strengths is the ability to communicate through different means, the most powerful one being speech. The words we choose can either fill people with joy and happiness or burn holes in their heart. Can you think of a moment in your life when someone said something exquisite to you? Take a moment and revisit that experience. How do you feel? There is more to language than grammar and spelling. It is capable of creating a whole range of emotions and feelings, which could be the difference between someone loving their life or hating it; building it up or damaging it.

We are often unaware of the fact that our words have a tremendous impact on our lives. Not only do our words determine our relationships with the people around us, but they also play a significant role in the quality of our relationship with the person we see when we look into the mirror. I am talking about the conversations we have with ourselves all the time: self-talk. Our brain responds to our verbal suggestions instantly, because they come from us.

So, if you are in the habit of beating yourself up all the time, saying things like, 'You are meant to fail', 'You can never be successful', 'You are an ugly duckling', 'You'd better stay within your limits; don't dream big', 'It's not meant for you', 'You are not intelligent enough', 'You are too old for this', the mind takes these suggestions as commands and continues creating a similar reality for you. The quality of your external and internal dialogue determines the quality of your life. Whenever we stop being mindful of what we say, the Secret Saboteur uses this constant stream of self-talk to hurt us.

Language impacts our lives in more ways than we can imagine. What if I were to say that from today, every word that you utter, internally or externally, will come true instantly? How would that change your language? In fact, if that were the case, most people would stop talking altogether, isn't it? Luckily, that is not the case.

But believe it or not, words do have the potential to turn into our realities, if used over and over. What we say is made of nothing other than vibrations that carry frequencies and the universe is a sea of vibrations, where everything is available. As I mentioned previously, vibrations that have matching frequencies are attracted towards each other. So our words will attract similar realities in our life.

Language is an automatic programme in us, which is why we treat our words so lightly. We utter most words unconsciously, out of habit. Little do we realize that we are constantly using language to transform our beliefs into reality. The words we say to other people and the words we say to ourselves add up and create our personal reality.

We all know that our thoughts influence our reality. But what influences our thoughts? Our daily conversations, both internal and external. Our language influences the way we think. As children, our thinking expands as our knowledge of language expands. This is why it's a good idea to keep building up our vocabulary and learning new words, as this helps expand our thinking and create new ideas.

Our life is all about patterns. We have a sleep pattern, we have a thinking pattern, we have an eating pattern, we have a behaviour pattern and we even have an emotional pattern. Similarly, we also have a language pattern. A pattern is something that is repeated and unconscious, like a habit. So if your language pattern is self-sabotaging and disempowering, you will encounter similar realities in your life and if it is affirmative and empowering, so will be your reality.

I remember when I was a child, people around me called me fat and dark. I was plump and not very fair, which should have been fine, but they called me these things as though it somehow made me inferior. This became a constant form of ridicule that was thrown at me all throughout my adolescence. I heard these words so frequently that I started believing that I was indeed ugly and not good enough. This was my interpretation of the words people used to describe me. This played havoc with my self-esteem and self-image and I turned into an extremely shy person, someone who had zero confidence, someone who was very uncomfortable with her body, someone who did not want to be around people. This eventually led to depression.

The words from the outside world created a belief inside me, which caused me to perceive myself as someone who was unworthy and unacceptable, which in turn caused me to have extremely damaging conversations with myself. It was a vicious cycle, a continuous negative loop, which is difficult for most people to come out of.

I had to put in a lot of mindful effort and work on myself to get out of this zone and see myself as a worthy and beautiful person. I was lucky enough to come out of it and change my language patterns entirely. This change helped me create immense positive changes in my life and I could see how my reality changed with it. Today, when I work with people from all walks of life, the first thing that helps me gauge their life is their language.

One of my clients, Suraj, could not complete his education because of his family circumstances. However, he did manage to secure a good life by starting a small retail shop. Financially, he was doing well, but there was a constant feeling of hurt and sadness inside him. When I first had a conversation with him, here's how it went (pay attention to his language):

Suraj: I don't like this feeling. I constantly feel like a failure. I wanted to complete my education, but because of my poor background, I couldn't. Had I been well educated, I would have been more successful. I don't like always feeling like a failure. When I look around me, I see all my cousins doing so well in life because they are more educated than I am. If I had had the privilege of getting a proper education, I would have started my own company.

Me: You can complete your education even now.

Suraj: I should have started that a long time back. Now I am too old. How I wish I had put in some more efforts earlier, then life would have been so much better.

As you will have noticed, his language shows that he operated from the victim mode, blaming the world and the circumstances for his current state. His entire focus was on what he didn't like or want in his life. So, the first thing I did with him was to make him work on changing his language, as that's the best way to change someone's thinking patterns. I gave him a few exercises that helped him work on his self-sabotaging language pattern.

The first thing he had to do was change his language to what he liked or wanted in life. For instance, instead of saying 'I don't like to always feel like a failure', saying 'I want to feel successful and happy'. Instead of 'I am too old,' 'I am excited' or 'There is no age limit to learning' and so on. Initially, it was not easy, because just like any other habit, breaking one's language pattern is also challenging. He took up the challenge to work on his language, and catch himself when he indulged in self-loathing and blaming. He would instantly change his internal or external dialogue to a more empowering one.

About a year after the completion of my programme, he called me one day and told me that he had created a business plan after completing a small course on business management and had also secured a loan for his new venture. His happiness knew no bounds – I could sense it in his voice and, of course, his language.

We always feel that creating great and big results in life requires a lot of hard work and effort. Although this is indeed a great method, sometimes it's just a small shift you need to make to achieve the same level of results. In Suraj's case, the shift in his language helped him change his deep-rooted limiting beliefs.

> ***'Language exerts hidden power, like the moon on the tides.'***
>
> ***– Rita Mae Brown***

There are certain words that we need to be careful while using and, if possible, limit their usage. Some of these words include 'should', 'must', 'have to', 'try', and 'not'.

These words take the power away from you. For instance, 'should', 'must', and 'have to' create a lot of pressure and guilt in us. Compare saying 'I should exercise more' or 'I have to exercise more' with saying 'I am excited to exercise more' or 'I can exercise more'. The latter instantly change the way you feel about exercise. It doesn't feel like a compulsion anymore. If I start saying, 'I am excited to ...' repeatedly, I shall end up feeling excited every time I plan to exercise. So replace your 'should', 'must', and 'have to' with 'could', 'can', and 'excited'. You will notice how your attitude and eventually your life start changing.

Similarly, 'not' is a word we need to get rid of. So often we end up telling ourselves, 'Oh, this is not possible', 'This is not my cup of tea', etc. 'Not' is a word that limits us like no other. It makes us believe that our capabilities are limited. Statistics reveal that parents of young children aged between two to eight years, end up saying 'No' to their children thousands of times. 'No, baby, do not throw it like that', 'Do not go near water', 'Don't jump from there', etc. These are statements that condition children to believe that they have limitations. So, instead of saying 'This is not possible', we can choose to say, 'This looks challenging right now.' Instead of telling the child 'Do not go near water', you can choose to say something like, 'Baby, wait – let's both go for swimming later today' or anything else that does not limit us or our children.

Another such word is 'try'. Now this is a really tricky one. A few days back, I was reading an article where the author had shared his experience visiting different tribes in Africa. When he visited the Swahili people, an ethnic group in East Africa, he received an extremely warm welcome. While bidding adieu to them, they invited him for dinner the next day, to which he said, 'I'll try.' His interpreter fell silent upon this and looked confused. When the author asked him what was wrong, he replied that he had suddenly realized that there was no word for 'try' in Swahili. So you could either say 'Yes' or 'No'. The author then told them that he would come.

This small story is so powerful and profound. Imagine if there were no word such as 'try', how our life would change. When we say 'try', we are once again rendering ourselves powerless; we leave everything to chance when we use this word. This is a word that makes us indecisive, weak, and ineffective. There is no 'trying'; you either do it or you don't – anything in between is a place of doubt, hesitation, and ambiguity.

Another crucial thing I want to cover in this chapter are the two words that create our identities: 'I am'. Our identity is how we perceive ourselves, how we define who we are, what we believe about ourselves consciously or unconsciously. Let me give you a small exercise here. Take a piece of paper and pen and write down what your definition of yourself is – who are you?

I am sure most of the statements you have written start with 'I am', like, 'I am beautiful', 'I am a senior executive', etc.

What we think we can or cannot do, what we consider possible or impossible is rarely a function of our true capability. It is actually a function of our identity. How we define ourselves, what we think about ourselves, and how we identify ourselves dictate all our behaviours, actions, and habits. However, we did not consciously choose our identity.

It is the result of: what other people have said about us (like in my case, 'fat' and 'dark'), significant events in our life, and other things that occurred without our awareness or approval.

A few years back, I was working with a girl who was addicted to drugs. She had completely recovered earlier but had relapsed. During my counselling sessions with her, I noticed her language and realized that she always said, 'I am a drug addict'. I saw that she had formed an identity of being a drug addict, though unconsciously. When we start identifying as someone (a drug addict in this case), our behaviour gets dictated by that identity. So, since she had started identifying herself as a drug addict, she relapsed. It was a self-fulfilling prophecy.

My challenge now was to shift her belief from 'I am a drug addict' to 'I have developed a drug addiction'. We worked towards creating a new, empowering identity for her by working on her ingrained subconscious limiting beliefs. Her self-recovery journey begun and within a couple of months, she had completely recovered. She went on to pursue her MBA from a reputed institute and ended up creating the life she had always dreamt of.

Someone who believes she has 'developed a drug addiction' can clearly change as opposed to one who believes herself to *be* a drug addict. She created a new identity – that of a 'leader', a 'contributor' – and ended up becoming a success story.

As we develop new beliefs about who we are, our behaviours, actions, and habits will change to support the new identity, and language plays a significant role in changing our current beliefs.

One of the most powerful and easiest ways to recognize what is our current identity code is to be aware of how we use our 'I am' statements. If you catch yourself saying something like 'I am depressed' or 'I am angry', understand that 'depressed' and 'angry' are part of your current identity and you might be creating circumstances in your life that make you more depressed or angry.

Whenever you say the words 'I am', the words that follow are a declaration, a statement that your subconscious mind treats as a command. So, statements like 'I am broke', 'I am fat', or 'I am confused' will be treated as commands by your subconscious mind, with you not even knowing that they have become a part of you and your reality.

So, it is very important to reframe these 'I am' statements and use them in an empowering way. Instead of 'I am angry' reframe it as 'I am feeling angry'. A feeling does not last forever, and a slight change in your language will create a massive shift in the quality of your life. We can use this technique to create new identity codes, codes that are resonant with our desires and aspirations, such as 'I am beautiful', 'I am successful', 'I am unstoppable', etc. When we consciously make an effort to change our 'I am' statements, we create a new identity of the person we want to become.

Another important facet of language that I want to talk about is the use of positive and affirmative statements. These are also called affirmations. What happens when we speak to ourselves in a positive and affirmative way repeatedly? These affirmations may not be true when we begin but with repetition, they sink into our subconscious mind, and we really start believing them and eventually they become our reality.

So, create a list of positive statements or phrases that describe how you want to be, how you want to live and read them out loud to yourself with emotions and expressions every day and you will experience a magical shift in your behaviour, habits and actions, which will help you create the life you want.

This reminds me of a gentleman who was part of my long-term programme. He was a business man who wanted to take his business to greater heights. However, despite all his efforts his revenues and profits were not going up. This had left him frustrated. I found that his beliefs about money were pessimistic. He made statements such as 'Money is hard to make', 'Money always eludes me', 'No matter how hard I try, I fail.' When I pointed this out, initially he was reluctant to accept that something as small as these statements could be hindering his growth. But eventually, he decided to work on changing his language. I asked him to carry a small writing pad and pen with him all the time and write down any thought that was despairing. I also told him to write down anything negative that he caught himself saying in the next one month. Then I told him to flip all the negative statements and write positive ones next to them. Then take a fresh piece of paper and write only the positive ones on it and destroy the one with the negative statements. I told him, 'Read the positive statements out loud to yourself every day without fail.' Some of the new statements about money that he wrote were 'Money comes to me easily and effortlessly', 'Money is easy to earn',

'I love money and money loves me.' Believe it or not, even though he had initially found this exercise ridiculous, he runs a multi-crore business today and affirmations have become an integral part of his life.

Remember, our language creates self-fulfilling prophecies. Your mind and body will follow where your words lead. So speak words that you want to turn into your reality. Focus on the things that you want in your life instead of blaming yourself or others or circumstances and become very conscious of your self-talk. The moment you catch yourself speaking to yourself or others in a disempowering way, immediately change your words and keep doing this until it becomes a habit. Switch your limiting language, such as *I can't, I don't, I won't*, to language of empowerment, such as *I can, I will, I choose, I love, I enjoy*. Notice how magically you and your life will change for the better.

> ***'Words have power. Use the language of leadership versus the vocabulary of a victim.'***
>
> ***– Robin Sharma***

We have covered four ideas so far to take charge of your life. The next idea is my favourite. It would not be an exaggeration to call it the most powerful tool to become the master of your life.

11

THE GIFT OF EMOTIONAL MASTERY*

How to heal yourself when you are hurt?

Relationships are the fundamental building blocks of our life. When we form connections with the people around us, there are bound to be disagreements, clashes, arguments, and conflicts. Such interactions leave us feeling a deep sense of hurt, sadness and confusion, which could ultimately lead to anger, frustration, guilt, or even hatred. These are all emotional wounds. Besides troubles in relationships, we face many failures, setbacks, and challenges in our life, which often take a toll on our emotional health.

These emotional wounds are as painful as physical wounds, sometimes even worse. If we leave all these emotional wounds

* This title and topic are inspired from the book called *Emotional First Aid* by Guy Winch.

untreated, it can lead to complications such as shame, chronic helplessness, and even clinical depression. But we do that with emotional injuries all the time.

This is because we do not prioritize our emotional health.

We all know how to take care of our physical wounds and can ascertain whether the wound can heal on its own or if we need a doctor or first aid. We know for sure how to make the physical wound heals. However, we unfortunately have no idea how to heal our emotional wounds. We all sustain them and they are as much a part of our life as the occasional scraped knee. We don't have a first-aid kit to take care of our emotional wounds.

Why is our physical health so much more important to us than our psychological or emotional health?

This is primarily because most of us don't know that emotional wounds exist. Secondly, even when people know they are wounded, they do not know how to heal emotional wounds. But the fact is that we sustain psychological injuries more often than physical ones. Just the way a simple cold can turn into a serious case of pneumonia if not treated in time, psychological injuries can also get worse if we keep ignoring them. They can lead to conditions like chronic depression, suicidal tendencies, and other grave mental illnesses. Emotional wounds can lead to many physical ailments as well. Just like our physical well-being, our mental well-being too is our responsibility.

Let's first understand what causes these emotional wounds. We all want certain things from the people in our life (family, friends, colleagues), but when we don't get that from them, we feel emotionally wounded.

Preeti went through a tormenting divorce after being married for twenty years. This traumatic experience left her emotionally wounded. After giving the prime years of her youth to her ex-husband and children, she found herself, lonely and rejected. She was lucky as far as her financial freedom was concerned, as she had never stopped working and also received a hefty alimony. Apart from that, she felt as if she was the biggest loser. She was emotionally battered. When we face rejections like the kind Preeti did, they cause emotional pain which is unbearable and destabilizes our fundamental feeling of belonging.

Some rejections are comparatively mild and, like a small scratch, heal with time. But when left untreated, even small wounds can get infected and lead to serious problems. When people in a study were asked to compare the pain of rejection to physical pain, they rated their emotional pain as equal in severity to that associated with natural childbirth and cancer treatments.

Rejection hurts the most when it comes from people we are close to and expect will treat us well. It hurts less when it comes from people we despise or people we are not acquainted with (like fans booing sportspeople when they lose); nevertheless, in either case, rejection hurts. Rejections often trigger aggressive behaviour and one feels a powerful urge to lash out, especially at those who rejected us. This is one of the primary reasons behind violence between romantic partners; many incidents of violence trigger from jealousy and suspicion of infidelity, which are deeply related to feelings of rejection.

Various studies concerning school shootings in the US have revealed that a majority of these incidents involved perpetrators who had experienced significant rejection and exclusion from schoolmates. In many cases, shooters specifically targeted students who had bullied, teased, or rejected them in the past. We are all wired with a fundamental need to belong, to feel accepted by others, and when this basic need is not met, it can have a detrimental effect on our physical and mental health.

Akshay lost his job at a telecom company. His entire department was fired as part of a cost-cutting measure, yet he took this rejection personally. He felt abandoned by his long-time colleagues, which made him feel unwanted. He thus avoided keeping contact with anyone, especially from his office. His ex-colleagues and friends tried to reach out to him, but he didn't respond to emails, phone calls, and messages that were sometimes about new job opportunities. After several months, his friends stopped reaching out to him, further validating the belief in Akshay's mind that they never cared about him. This left him feeling lonely and even more dejected.

This happens with most people who face rejections of some kind and end up taking them personally. In Akshay's case, he ignored the fact that it was not only he who had been fired and took it personally, which lead to making him feeling worse. He was left with a lot of resentment, anger, sadness, and his self-esteem went for a toss.

There are so many Preetis and Akshays around us and maybe we too are or were in that place at some point. Rejection and loneliness are two major factors that cause deep psychological wounds – as in Preeti's and Akshay's cases – wounds that distort our perceptions and cloud our thinking.

Wounds like these make you believe that those around you care much less than they actually do. They make you fearful of reaching out, because you are afraid of setting yourself up for rejection and heartache again when your heart is already hurting more than you can stand. You end up feeling lonely even with people surrounding you all day.

There's a lot of research on loneliness and all of it is alarming. It won't just make you miserable, it can even kill you. Chronic loneliness increases your likelihood of early death by 14 per cent, concluded John Cacioppo, who studied loneliness in depth at the University of Chicago.[1] It causes high blood pressure and high cholesterol; it suppresses the functioning of your immune system, making you vulnerable to all kinds of illnesses and diseases.

A year after her divorce, Preeti was ready for her first date. She had decided to move on and give love another chance. She met a man through an online dating site. He was successful and good-looking. Based on their initial online conversations, he seemed really into her. This gave her the courage to take the next step. After a long time, she was excited, so she bought a new dress, used makeup and hairstyled by a stylist. She then met her date at an upscale bar for a drink. After exchanging initial pleasantries, they chatted about different subjects and had a great time. It seemed like most of their interests were aligned. She came back home after exchanging numbers in high spirits, hoping for a new and healthier relationship.

A day, two days, a week passed by, but there was no call or message from the man. Preeti was tempted to call or ping him, but she did not want to seem needy. The man never contacted her again. She checked his profile again on the dating site: it was not there anymore. She was felt extremely dispirited and could not understand what had gone wrong.

She was devastated and confided in a friend to find some solace. Here's what her friend said: 'What else did you expect? Look at you. You look old and tired. You are divorced. You are overweight, you don't have anything interesting to talk about. Why would a handsome and successful man like him ever go out with a loser like you? You deserve to be deserted, you are not worthy of love; that's why your husband of twenty years rejected you.'

Shocking! To think that a friend could be so cruel!

Don't be so shocked. Let me tell you the truth now. It wasn't the friend who said all that, because real friends don't talk to us like that, do they? It was Preeti who said all this to herself. That's something we all do, especially after a rejection. We start thinking about all our shortcomings, our imperfections, the things we wish we were, what we wish we weren't, and we call ourselves names.

A rejection leaves us with emotional scars that destroy our self-esteem, leave us feeling emotionally isolated. What we need to understand is that our self-esteem has already been eroded by the rejection. By bullying ourself, we damage it even further. It is like trying to treat a bump on the head by hitting yourself with a hammer. Insane.

Ranveer, a top sales executive in an advertising agency, had a dream of starting his own enterprise. After fifteen years of experience, he decided to finally take the plunge. He was courageous enough to invest a major chunk of his savings in his new startup. He was a star performer in his company, so when he handed in his resignation, his boss offered him the chance to come back whenever he wanted.

Like any new business, he faced a lot of challenges. Initially, he kept going and did not give up. He was enthusiastic and ready to face all the hurdles, or so he believed. One year into the business, he had exhausted all his investments and the revenues were still not great. He could not even break even. He went from one investor to another to obtain funds but somehow could not get any investments to support his startup. This left him dejected and broken. Failure after failure was breaking him from within. He felt guilty for having put his family's future at stake for his dream. He decided to get back to his job and focus on supporting his family.

'Having given up on my dream is killing me. I tried my best to make it work but I failed. I can never be a business owner. I have no choice but to accept it and move on. Can you help me accept this fact, as I'm finding it hard to do so on my own,' Ranveer said after sharing his story with me.

Failure is the third biggest factor that inflicts emotional wounds, after rejection and loneliness. Like rejection, it damages our self-esteem by making us doubt our abilities, capabilities, and skills. It saps our optimism, motivation, and confidence, as in Ranveer's case. It makes us feel helpless and trapped, thus unconsciously triggering stress, anxiety, and fears that immobilize us and sabotage our future efforts. So we end up saying, 'I don't have it in me. Never in the future will I try something like this again.' When failures come one after the other, we tend to feel like we have exhausted all our options. Failure makes us lose hope and feel trapped. Then we feel that the only option left is to give up on our dreams.

If we miss the promotion we were expecting and thought we deserved for having worked so hard, we stop making an effort, because we now start believing that the boss is not going to promote us anyway. If we fail to lose weight in the first month of exercising, we conclude that we can never get fitter, so we stop exercising altogether. Failure has the power to convince us that we have no chance of getting what we want, so we simply stop trying.

Ranveer's failure left him befuddled. He was convinced that he was not meant to be what he wanted to be. That's what failure does to us; it tricks our mind into believing that we cannot achieve our dreams. Your mind now tries to convince you that you are not capable of something. If you believe it, you start feeling helpless and give up too soon or not try at all. This will convince you even further that you cannot succeed. It's a vicious cycle. This is why so many people function below their actual potential. Somewhere along the way, sometimes a single failure, sometimes failure after failure, convinced them that they could not succeed and they believed it. Believing means being convinced of something and once our mind is convinced, it's difficult to change it. It is natural to feel demoralized and defeated after a failure, but you cannot allow yourself to become convinced that you won't succeed. You have to learn to gain control over the situation; you have to break the vicious circle before it begins.

Here, I would like to talk about a habit that worsens our emotional wounds. It is the habit of replaying the same distressing situations, memories, and feelings over and over again. This is like repeatedly scratching your physical wounds. This will only aggravate the wound, and it could even get infected. If you continue digging and scratching, you might also end up losing that body part. This is true about our emotional wounds as well.

Everyone at the party was laughing at you, or your boss yelled at you in the meeting in front of your colleagues, or the teacher made you feel stupid in class, or you had a bad fight with your best friend. And you just can't stop replaying these scenes in your head for days, sometimes for weeks on end. Pondering about upsetting events in this way is actually a habit – a bad habit. This habit has an adverse effect, because when we spend so much time focusing on upsetting and negative thoughts, we are actually putting ourselves at a significant risk of developing clinical depression, alcoholism, impaired problem-solving, eating disorders, and even cardiovascular diseases.

However, the good news is that this a habit and, just like any other bad habit, it can be changed. People who suffer from this habit have the strong urge to continue, but studies tell us that even a small two-minute distraction is sufficient to break this urge in that moment. So, the next time you catch yourself wanting to replay worrying, upsetting, and negative thoughts, force yourself to focus on something pleasant for at least two minutes and you will see the urge pass. That takes care of the immediate short-term handling of the issue.

Now, let us look at how to heal and cure emotional wounds.

When we encounter rejection, loneliness, or failure, we end up with an emotional wound that affects our thinking, floods us with anger and resentment, erodes our self-esteem and confidence, saps our motivation and optimism, immobilizes us, and causes us to believe that we are not worthy of our dreams. However, just as we have the power to heal our physical wounds, we also have the power and the ability to heal our emotional wounds. There are many ways in which we can do this. Let's look at the simplest and most effective ways of creating emotional well-being.

One, we need to acknowledge that we are emotionally wounded and that we are feeling overwhelming emotions. This acceptance will, in fact, start the healing process.

Two, we need to learn techniques that can help regulate our emotions like anger, resentment, hatred, guilt, or remorse. One highly effective technique is to 'reframe' the painful event in our minds. This technique helps change the meaning of the event to one that is less infuriating or less painful. In the case of Preeti's date, what Preeti needs to do first is to tell herself, 'Okay, I know I am hurt. I am angry at him for rejecting me like this, but now I choose to take this as a sign that someone even better, someone more loving, is waiting for me. Had he not rejected me, I would have lost out on the chance of meeting someone even better, someone who would love me for who I am.'

Or, in Akshay's case, what he needs to tell himself is, 'Okay, I know that I feel a deep sadness and a strange sense of betrayal, I feel lonely and left out, which is all fine. From now on, I choose to think that the loss of my job is a sign from the universe to start looking for a job that will offer me a bigger and better position, because I deserve bigger and better.'

Changing the implication of setbacks like these is one of the most powerful and effective ways of dealing with emotional turmoil.

Three, 'give' when you feel the need to 'receive' the most. When working on healing your emotional wounds, one of the best ways is to help others. Helping others could mean anything from volunteer work, visiting cancer patients, old-age homes or orphanages, to something as simple as helping your loved ones with important tasks, such as helping kids with their homework or helping your spouse with his or her chores. You will be surprised by how giving reduces your emotional pain; it works like a medicine in tending to your psychological wounds.

Four, we need to work on building and protecting our damaged self-esteem. The best way to do this is to work on developing self-love. Self-love comes when we learn the art of silencing the inner critic within our mind, telling us things like Preeti's did to hers after she was rejected the second time. Stop blaming yourself; stop pulling yourself down; stop beating yourself up for someone else's actions. Even if it was your mistake, it doesn't mean that there is anything wrong with you. Who doesn't make mistakes? Take the lessons from your mistakes and move on. I will share a small exercise here that can help you develop self-love.

- *Choose one event in your life where you have experienced a failure, embarrassment, humiliation or rejection, which made you feel bad and self-critical.*
- *Imagine the same event happening to your dearest friend. Now, write a letter to this friend with the purpose of making him/her feel better about himself/herself. Express your kindness, understanding, and genuine concern and remind him/her of his/her qualities and abilities. Tell him/her why he/she is so important and worthy of love and compassion, without being judgemental. For example, if you are writing to Preeti, tell her that even though her date never called her back, which was a fact, this did not mean that Preeti was a loser or not good*

enough. The latter would be judgemental and non-factual. So, don't judge yourself based on someone else's actions.

- *Now, go back to the event and read this letter out to yourself, as if you had written it to yourself. This letter will help you to build self-love, as you will now see yourself in a new light.*

Another simple way to build self-esteem is to write yourself a love letter every week. This love letter should emphasize your attributes and qualities, including achievements that are significant and meaningful to you. Aim for at least ten qualities.

A third way is this: Look into the mirror every day and tell your reflection that you love yourself. These seemingly simple actions are actually extremely effective.

When we make mistakes or when someone hurts us, only then we have low self-esteem; do we perceive it as a sign that they don't like us or that they disrespect us. When we develop self-love, this perception will die a natural death.

Lastly, we need to learn the art of forgiveness. Forgive the people, situations, and circumstances that caused you emotional pain. Forgiving is important because otherwise we continue holding on to emotional pains and wounds that can get worse if we don't forgive. Forgiveness is important for our emotional health. Don't forgive because the other person or situation deserves forgiveness (because they might not deserve it); forgive because you deserve happiness and good emotional health. Forgiving oneself for past mistakes is also a crucial component in achieving self-love.

By giving when you feel lonely, changing your response to failures, protecting your self-esteem, and battling negative thinking, you will not only heal your emotional wounds but you will also build emotional immunity, resilience.

The world would be a beautiful place if there was no depression and loneliness, if people knew how to deal with failures, felt great about themselves, and were more empowered and felt happier and fulfilled.

Imagine what the world would be like if everyone was emotionally and mentally healthier. That's the world we all deserve, so let's build that world together.

> ***'Healing doesn't mean the damage never existed;***
> ***It means the damage no longer controls our lives.'***
>
> – ***Akshay Dubey***

So, become a master of your emotions and you will see how all the areas of your life will start improving. You can develop this skill. I promise you this one change will change everything for good.

12

THE IRRITABILITY CURE

What lies beneath your anger?

Holi was around the corner. Monali had a very important meeting with a prospective client that day. If things went well, it would mean a major business leap. As she walked towards her car in the parking, a big balloon of coloured water fell on her head. Monali was furious and let out some not-so-nice words. When she looked up to shout at the person some more, she found that the person had disappeared. Her clothes were all wet and colour-stained. There was no way she could go to office like that. She had to rush back and change her clothes; all the while, she was angry and muttered curses at that person.

She entered her office, still grumpy. The incident had made her snappy and did not allow her to focus on her work. She went for the meeting in the same emotional state, angry, irritated, and lashing out at whoever came in her way. As a result, she was not at her best and did not form a good rapport with her clients. In fact, she ended up arguing with them. Not surprisingly, she could not crack the deal. That one annoying incident in the morning ended up becoming a major disappointment in Monali's life.

Many of us go through similar situations in our everyday life, where we allow our anger to get the better of us. Anger can be caused by both internal and external events. One could be angry at a person or an event (like a fight with a loved one or getting stuck in a traffic jam) or one could feel anger because of worrying about one's personal issues or ruminating about past hurtful memories.

Anger is an emotional state that varies in intensity from mild irritation to intense fury or rage, according to Charles Spielberger, a psychologist who specializes in the study of anger.[1] The instinctive way to express anger is to respond aggressively, since anger, like fear, is our natural response to threats, which allows us to either fight or protect ourselves when attacked. So, a certain amount of anger is necessary for our survival. However, we cannot physically lash out at every person or situation that irritates us. After all, there are laws and social norms that limit how far we can take our anger. Though it is natural to feel angry, and sometimes even furious, in unpleasant and irritating situations, the fact is that we cannot completely avoid such people or situations.

So the important question here is: *How do we handle our anger?*

According to Dr Spielberger, anger can either be expressed, supressed, or calmed.

Expressing your anger assertively is the healthiest way to express it; however, if done aggressively, it can be detrimental. Being assertive means being respectful of yourself and others. It is beneficial to express anger assertively by learning how to make your needs clear or have them be met without hurting others.

When anger is suppressed, it can be redirected towards others, as in Monali's case, or it can turn inwards. This can be harmful, causing hypertension, high blood pressure, or depression. Besides this, unexpressed anger can create other problems like passive–aggressive behaviour or a personality that is cynical or hostile.

Finally, learning the art of calming down when anger strikes is the most difficult but the most useful of all three. This can be done by taking steps to lower your heart rate (using meditation or yoga) and let the feeling subside on its own.

However, there is more to anger than just learning how to deal with it effectively. This 'something' is what I will be covering in this chapter. People, circumstances, or memories that make you angry are actually a way for the universe to reveal to you your weaknesses, fears, and false and limiting beliefs.

> ***'Everything that irritates us about others can lead us to an understanding of ourselves.'***
>
> ***– Carl Jung***

Things that make us angry and frustrated are the very things that when seen from a different perspective, will help us pinpoint exactly what is holding us back from living a fulfilling life. This understanding can help us evolve as a person. They are the signposts to what we need to work on and the fears and doubts that we need to face.

I remember a client I had a couple of years back, Asheesh, who was a senior executive in an MNC and was doing really well professionally. However, his biggest complaint was that no one in his workplace seemed to like him. Most of his peers maintained a healthy distance from him. Although professionally they were cordial and supportive, there was no interaction at a personal level whatsoever. This made him feel isolated and lonely.

My interactions with him made it very clear to me that Asheesh had no close friendships – not only in his office but also in his personal life. I wanted to know why people hesitated to be friendly with him. After a series of coaching sessions with him, I realized that he had a habit of misinterpreting things and holding grudges. There were many incidents that he shared with me that pointed at this habit, but Asheesh was not aware of this behaviour. For example, he told me how he had once overheard his colleagues talking ill about him behind his back.

'So, then what did you do?' I asked.

'Nothing. I just stopped interacting with them.'

When I asked him if he was 100 per cent sure they were talking about him, he said he was not sure but that there was no one else they could be talking about. He did not stop to enquire whether they were indeed talking about him and wrongly concluded that the conversation was about him. He had a habit of jumping to conclusions without checking the facts, and then holding grudges against people for these imagined wrongs. I asked him just one question: 'What if they were talking about someone else, and suddenly they find you behaving weirdly with them. Do you think they would want to be around you, then?' He said he had never considered that possibility. He then suddenly realized a pattern.

A pattern that prevented people from befriending him. For who would want to be friends with someone who always misinterpreted things and then holds grudges? People are already dealing with a lot of stress, and no one would want to add another stressor in their lives.

The reason I share Asheesh's story here is to emphasize how anger can help us uncover some of our limiting and self-sabotaging behaviours. Asheesh realized that his anger was unjustified when he analyzed the root of his anger. He discovered his unproductive pattern of jumping to conclusions.

In Asheesh's case he was angry with a situation created by his own imagination. However, we might encounter situations or people who deliberately hurt us or abuse us, leaving us angry.

Sandeep, a marketing executive, was handling an important marketing campaign. He and his team had done a fabulous job and the campaign was a massive success. Sandeep was now expecting praise from his boss and a promotion, as it was long overdue. However, his colleague and partner in the campaign, Rajat, who had done much less work, ended up getting all the accolades for the success and was promoted instead of Sandeep. This left Sandeep angry and bitter.

His anger here was completely justified. He was the one who had put in all the hard work and extra hours and then someone else had reaped the rewards. When Sandeep shared his story with me, I found that Sandeep was humble and never spoke about his contributions. This had given Rajat the opportunity to take the lead and talk about his work with their boss whenever he got a chance. As I continued working with Sandeep, I found that he believed that 'actions speak louder than words', so there was no need for him to speak about his contributions.

Having a belief like this is not inherently bad, but one also has to realize that if we don't speak for ourselves, no one else will. Sandeep had a pattern of extreme humility, which was costing him. There is a very popular phrase which says, 'Too much of anything is bad.' Here, excessive humility was proving bad for Sandeep. I could see his limiting pattern, but that was not enough. This had to be brought to his awareness. So I asked him to do a simple introspective exercise. I asked him to take some alone time and ask himself the following questions and write down the answers honestly:

- *What is this situation trying to teach me?*
- *What is the hidden fear/belief/pattern/behaviour that is making me feel so angry in this moment?*

- *Is this anger about this person or situation, or is it something about me that I need to figure out and address?*

A few days later, he requested me to meet him. He shared that these three questions helped him see a side of his personality that he had not been aware of. He had realized that his overtly humble nature was allowing other people to sabotage his success. He said that when he started writing the answers to these questions, especially the last one, he understood that he was angry because he had never had the courage to stand up and speak for himself. Had he assertively done that, he would have surely gotten the promotion.

This happens with so many of us: someone else takes the credit for our hard work and walks away with all the rewards, causing a lot of anger and hurt. This is when it's time to introspect and ask yourself questions that will unravel the hidden and sabotaging pattern or behaviour causing the pain.

I have created a simple introspective exercise that helps people get to the root of their anger and choose a response that serves them. So, whenever you encounter a situation or a person that makes you angry, take a deep breath, pause, and ask yourself:

- *Is this worth my energy?*
- *What is this person/situation trying to teach me?*
- *What is the hidden fear/belief/pattern that is making me feel so angry in this moment?*

- *I know this anger is not about this person or situation; it's something about me that I need to figure out and address. What is it?*
- *If I react, will that help me?*
- *What response, in this moment, can serve me?*
- *Will my getting angry solve any problem, or will it aggravate it?*
- *Is this really about me?*

This will help you uncover the hidden limiting patterns, behaviours, and habits that might be hindering your happiness and help you deal with anger effectively.

Let us go back to Monali's case. Had she chosen to pause and reflect on the root of her anger, she could have changed her emotional state and things could have turned out better. This self-enquiry could have made her realize that it was senseless to lose her cool and that the situation was teaching her to be more patient, forgiving, or accepting of others. Or maybe it was teaching her to just relax and look at the fun side of life and that maybe she was taking life too seriously. There was really nothing much to be done about a small, external, accidental event. So her best option was to look at it, take a few deep breaths to calm down and let it go; to look ahead and make the best of the coming hours. Who knows, had she chosen to introspect, the outcome could have been different!

Initially, it might all seem difficult, but if you practise this simple technique every time you face a similar situation, you will realize that in no time, you have mastered your anger. I always talk about *mastering* our emotions and not *managing* them. And mastery comes only with practice.

So, you can either blame people who trigger your anger and take it personally. Or you can be wise and look deeply into yourself to discover the reasons underlying your negative reactions.

> ***'I have learned silence from the talkative, toleration from the intolerant, and kindness from the unkind; yet, strange, I am ungrateful to those teachers.'***
>
> ***– Kahlil Gibran***

Remember that anger too is trying to teach us something. Something that is blocking our way to a happy and fulfilling life. When we introspect on what angers us, we can learn from it and move closer to the self we want to be. Are you willing to take the lesson?

13

PROCRASTINATION: BAD OR GOOD?*

Procrastination hampers our growth in a big way.

Has this ever happened to you? You sit down to do an important task with the intention of finishing it and suddenly find yourself looking at your phone the moment you get a notification. You then feel like checking your emails; you come across a mail with a catchy subject and decide to check it. You read the mail and find it interesting and want to know more, so you click on the links in the mail, which take you to different websites. Here you come across a gripping advertisement and you click on the link. Next thing you know, almost three hours have gone by and you haven't even started your task. Does this sound familiar? I bet it does!

* References in this chapter are inspired from an online course: 'Confessions of an ex procrastinator by Gregory Caremans – Brain Academy

This act of delaying or postponing a task or a set of tasks is called 'procrastination'.

Why do we procrastinate?

There are some misconceptions about it. Some people think that procrastinators are lazy. That is actually not the case. They are far from lazy. Procrastinators are often hard-working and multitasking. Because the task at hand is extremely boring they divert their attention on other things that seem interesting at the moment.

At the root of this behaviour are some 'unconscious drivers'. These are impulses we are not conscious of. As much as we would like to believe that we are rational beings, we are actually not. Yes, we have the ability to think rationally, but before that, we are emotional and social beings. All our decisions are not the result of our conscious logical self but of these unconscious drivers. So, what are these unconscious drivers and their resultant behaviours? Let's find out!

The very first unconscious driver is our *life experiences*, the beliefs and values that are coded in our brains, right from the day we were born. Procrastination isn't something we inherit from our parents. Other than genes, there are some other things that are passed on to us from our parents: the way we are brought up, what we see and learn as we grow up. Our life experiences can create various different responses in us.

In the 1980s, Esther Rothblum and her colleagues suggested that children with overtly critical, demanding parents might learn to avoid tasks, rather than risking failure.[1]

Their research shows a clear link between harsh controlling fathers and procrastinating children. The reason behind it apparently is that too much authority keeps children from developing the ability to regulate themselves, as they are told every single thing they should or should not do. So, in the long run, these kids don't get the opportunity to make their own decisions and to act independently. In these circumstances, they don't have many options and procrastinating can become a form of 'passive–aggressive rebellion'. Unfortunately, once they've become accustomed to procrastinating, once their brain is wired to this way of doing things it may stick with them for the rest of their lives.

Besides passive–aggressive rebellion, the other way a child with strong authoritarian upbringing can turn out is to be left with low self-esteem. The issue for procrastinators is that they just don't think they are capable of doing the task at hand. When parents are too strict, too controlling – 'Don't do this', 'Don't do that', 'Ask my permission first' – the message they are sending is interpreted by the child's brain as 'You are not capable enough.' So, as the years pass by, the child's brain gets wired not to take initiative, not knowing where to start or how to do things by themselves.

The other way our life's experiences – the unconscious driver of our behaviour – can lead to procrastination is through the need to be perfect. This makes perfectionists. A person who wants something to be perfect is never happy with the end result and is consequently always postponing and delaying deadlines in order to improve whatever they are working on. However, perfectionism never leads to perfection, so the result is that it takes forever to get things done.

Then there are 'adventure-seekers', people who say they need the pressure of a deadline to be able to produce their best work. This is a lie they tell themselves just to make them feel better about their procrastination. If you claim this, you obviously have no idea how your brain works. We don't work better when we are under stress. Quality work isn't produced overnight. Rome was not built in a day, as they say. What procrastinators are actually after is the thrill of completing an almost impossible task. This thrill is felt because of the brain releasing a neurotransmitter called dopamine, which is a feel-good chemical and is also associated with cocaine and gambling. So, it's this dopamine rush they are after.

The second unconscious driver is our *environment* or rather our responses to it.

The first category of procrastinators who come under this driver are the ones who cannot prioritize. Everything seems equally important to them. Of whatever the environment throws at them, they simply don't know how to differentiate between the urgent, the important and the stuff that can wait. It's all the same to them. So they end up failing deadlines or just not doing the things that matter, because something else came up. It's not that they don't want to do something, it's just that they are not good at planning and organization.

The second category of procrastinators under this driver are the ones addicted to something. This thing takes up all their time and they are consequently left with hardly any time to do anything else. People who are addicted to shopping, videogames, the internet, social media, or watching series, belong to this category. These addictive distractions in their environment cause them to procrastinate on what needs to be done. Whatever it is, it will always come after their addiction. It is not that they are avoiding a task; they are just too busy with their addiction to do anything else.

The third and final unconscious driver is our *basic survival instinct*. One of our primal instincts is to stay safe and one of the best strategies to stay safe is simply to avoid danger.

Early humans had many dangers that were threats to survival, such as wild animals, violent weather, lack of food and so on. But today, the danger is not a tiger but something as simple as a phone call we have to make or a conversation we should have. We know beforehand that it will be unpleasant, so our brain associates it with danger. Whether the danger is real or perceived, our brain associates it as an activity to be avoided, hence the procrastinating behaviour. So, whenever a task is seen as a threat (to one's comfort), the procrastinator, as a reaction, will stop acting altogether. It's purely a stress reaction.

All human behaviour is governed by only one simple principle and that is *to avoid pain and gain pleasure*. We have pain and pleasure associations in our brain for almost everything we know or do; based on the above three unconscious drivers, our life experiences, our response to environment, and our basic survival instinct, which drive all our behaviour –

procrastination, in this case. Sometimes these associations are detrimental to us. Let me explain using my mother's example.

My mother is diabetic. However, she is a huge fan of sweets. The moment she sees desserts, it's almost impossible to stop her. She is on medication, but still unable to stop herself from eating sweets despite her knowing that sweets are harmful for her. That's because sweets give her instant pleasure and gratification. Consuming sweets has a pleasure association in her brain, and hence the difficulty in changing that behaviour.

The same is true of procrastination. We exhibit this behaviour because we want instant gratification. Like in the earlier example, we end up drifting into tasks that are insignificant at the cost of something that is important, because it gives us instant pleasure. We all know the repercussions of such behaviour – it could be a drop in our performance or efficiency, a business loss, or it could even cost us our job. We still find ourselves struggling to change. This is because in our mind, we associate these irrelevant tasks with instant pleasure and important tasks have an association with instant pain. When I say instant pain, it means that the task seems like a burden in the present moment, although in the long run we know it would lead to pleasure. Another good example is the constant struggle to eat right, exercise, and stay fit – it is one area that most of us struggle with. Long-term rewards and consequences do not motivate us in the present.

We now have an idea about why we procrastinate. But is procrastination really bad? Before we explore the answer to this question, let us understand if we can redefine procrastination. I believe there are two types of procrastination:

1. Purposeless procrastination
2. Purposeful procrastination

Purposeless procrastination is the habit of putting off important tasks to work on irrelevant and unimportant stuff based on the three unconscious drivers. So far, what we have discussed belonged to this category.

Purposeful procrastination, on the other hand, is putting off working on irrelevant stuff to work on stuff that really matters. So, if you ask me, 'Is procrastination really bad?', I would say it is not – provided it belongs to the second category. All highly successful people fall in the latter category.

Many people ask me if there is a way to get rid of the habit of procrastination. My answer is 'No'. We all are procrastinators, but what matters is to which category we belong.

So, the key is to shift from purposeless procrastination to purposeful procrastination. How can we do that?

It's simple: by working on changing our pain and pleasure associations. If we could associate purposeless procrastination with pain in our mind, our behaviour would automatically shift to purposeful procrastination.

Rajesh had a very good relationship with his wife, Aarti. However, he was a purposeless procrastinator. This one habit was the only bone of contention between the two of them. On one occasion, it was about to take a permanent toll on their twelve-year marriage.

Aarti was returning home after visiting her parents for a month. Her flight had been delayed by two hours. She tried calling Rajesh to inform him about the delay, so he could come to the airport accordingly, but his phone was not reachable. She assumed he would check the arrival time himself. She landed around 11 p.m., and there was no sign of Rajesh. She tried calling him, but his number was still not reachable. She was now worried and she did not know what to do and whom to call at that hour. She waited at the airport till 12. Rajesh was still not reachable. Aarti was panicking by now. She decided to take a taxi home. Though the idea of taking a taxi at midnight in a city like Delhi was scary, she had no choice. She was angry, but more than that, she was worried about Rajesh.

She was worried and scared and recited the *Hanuman Chaleesa* non-stop as she sat in the taxi speeding through the city. At the same time, worrying thoughts buzzed in her head: 'I hope he is fine', 'Why is his mobile not reachable?', 'Why did he not come to pick me up?' She knew Rajesh was protective about her and would never want her to come home on her own at such an odd hour. All these thoughts made Aarti more and more restless. Her heart was pounding hard, and she was sweating with fear.

She got home around 1 a.m. Fearing the worst, she unlocked the main door and stepped into the foyer. She wanted more than anything to see Rajesh sleeping in their bedroom, fit and fine. With trembling hands, she opened the door of the bedroom. Rajesh was not there. She was now shaking with fear. She thought of checking their living room.

Rajesh was sleeping like a child on the sofa. She was relieved to see him fine. But then her anger surfaced. Why had he not come to pick her up? Why was his phone not reachable? Why did he not call her? All these questions now flooded her mind. Aarti was a wise and mature woman. She did not think it right to disturb her husband at that odd hour. So she just changed and went to sleep.

'Aarti, wake up, sweetheart.' Rajesh stroking her hair lovingly with a cup of tea in the other hand the next morning.

Aarti opened her eyes, still swollen and red from having cried herself to sleep last night.

'Oh, really? Am I your sweetheart?'

'I am so sorry, darling. I know I have committed an unforgivable mistake. Can you please forgive me?' Rajesh pleaded with guilt.

'Do you have any idea what I went through yesterday?' Aarti's throat almost choked and her eyes welled with tears. 'I was so worried for you. Your phone was not reachable. I kept calling you continuously like a maniac. Where were you? What happened to your phone? Why did you not come? I feared for your well-being. I could have died from fear. You know you are my life.' She was now crying like a baby.

Rajesh was speechless. He did not know what to say. His one mistake could have cost him the love of his life. He was now realizing the cost of his bad habit of purposeless procrastination. Last evening, when Rajesh had gotten back home, he had planned to leave for the airport after dinner. While eating, he had switched on the TV and seen that his favourite movie was playing on one of the channels. He thought he would watch it for some time and then leave, not realizing that his mobile's battery had died. He did not even realize going off to sleep while watching the movie.

'Tell me, Rajesh. Why?' Aarti was screaming now.

Rajesh told her honestly about what had happened. Aarti could not believe that Rajesh could push something so important for a movie.

'You know what, Rajesh, this habit of yours has always bothered me. But I thought you would work on it yourself. I have never tried to change anything about you, but this is an extreme. I don't think I can live with you anymore.' Aarti left from there.

It took Rajesh more than a month to pacify Aarti and bring her back. This is when he decided to change his habit for good. This experience associated so much pain with his habit of procrastination that Rajesh changed it in no time. So, one way to associate pain with purposeless procrastination is to go through a painful experience, as in Rajesh's case. But why wait for the repercussions of this behaviour to change?

So, how do we do this without having to face the bad consequences of this habit? Some of us might think that we have to develop willpower to be able to change these associations and thus the behaviour; many people believe that everything can be solved with willpower. However, in the case of procrastination, it isn't will power that is low, it's the temptation that is overwhelming. For Rajesh, the temptation to watch the movie was so great that he did not realize his phone was dead and that he needed to leave for the airport. Non-procrastinators do not have more willpower than procrastinators; they are just less tempted and the differentiating factors are the three unconscious drivers.

Well, then, if not willpower, then what will help change the sabotaging pain and pleasure associations? The answer is *motivation*. The one reason we always cite when we procrastinate is lack of motivation. How does one feel motivated all the time? This behaviour will not change if we do not feel motivated, will it? Then what is the way out?

This is one of the most common questions that people ask me: *How do we ensure that we stay motivated all the time?* So, here are eight ways that are highly effective in keeping us motivated. Let us explore them one by one.

1. *Take action*: The first step is very simple; action.
   Vivek has an important presentation to prepare. He has known this for weeks but has been putting it off day after day. He doesn't feel motivated enough to do it, though he feels a nagging pain and anxiety thinking about it – but the pain is not enough to nudge him into action. Then the day before the deadline comes. Now, the pain of inaction has reached the threshold of his tolerance and he completes the slides just hours before the presentation. He then feels relaxed and the pain is gone, too.

Did you notice that the moment he took action, the pain vanished and left him feeling relaxed (pleasure)! What if, instead of waiting for the pain to reach its threshold for us to take action, we just take action, even if we don't *feel* like doing it? Here, we are actively working on changing the association from pain to pleasure.

Procrastination actually leaves you feeling guilty, ashamed, and anxious, which is more painful than taking action. So the very first step is to *start*. Motivation comes *after* starting, not before; it's the natural outcome of action. Action takers are always motivated.

2. *Be with action takers*: So, how do we ensure that we take action? Simple again; surround yourself with people who are action takers. Our social environment has a huge impact on how we behave. We unconsciously tend to conform to group norms and behaviours. If you surround yourself with procrastinators, you are more likely to procrastinate. Likewise, if you surround yourself with people who are action takers, you will be more likely to take action yourself. So, choose wisely who you spend time with.

3. *Get a motivation pal*: Find someone close to you whom you can call whenever you are having a hard time getting motivated. Someone who can give you a pep talk to make you feel better and get on with your task. This person could be a friend, mentor, spouse – anyone who is a well-wisher.

Also, don't forget to celebrate with this pal whenever you complete a task you had been procrastinating.

4. *Create a motivation pack*: This is a strategy that is simple but very effective. If you don't like whatever you have to do, do it along with something you do like, such as listening to your favourite music while exercising. When you pack something you want to do with whatever you are procrastinating, you'll do them both. This is one of the most powerful ways to stay in action and do things that you dread doing.

5. *Change perception*: One of the issues with procrastination is that we think about the activity as being boring or difficult or really unpleasant. That's what we are anticipating and that's why we don't do it. Now, instead of thinking how horrible the activity is, start looking at the brighter side. See the 'bigger picture'. Change your perspective and find good things about the activity – how this activity will serve you well in the future. You don't have to lie to yourself; just focus on the good things and each time you think about the activity, force yourself to think about those positive aspects. While doing the activity, be mindful of its positive impact. The aim here is to change the way you look at the activity and actually, over time, start enjoying it. This is a powerful way to change the pain and pleasure associations in our brain.

6. *Change the environment*: This, again, is a very effective way to stay motivated to complete the task at hand. Anything can

serve as a distraction to a procrastinator. As we now know, the issue is not lack of willpower, it is too much temptation. So, remove these temptations from your environment. If your X-box is a problem, give it to your 'motivation pal', who will give you access only to celebrate whenever you complete a task. Create an environment where it is hard for you to fall into temptation. Keep a clean desk policy; block all your notifications when you are working. Make blocks of forty minutes of hard work and then take ten-minute breaks to check your messages or just take a walk or stretch and then continue.

7. *Create a compelling vision*: A vision is the reason we do things in the first place. A compelling vision is something that is so large, beautiful, and enticing that it means the world to you. Something you can't wait to see happen. You may have to fight to make it a reality, but the prospect of getting there is so wonderful that you are willing to take the hits for it. It's your Holy Grail, your Promised Land. Now, let me ask you. Do you have yours? Have you thought about it? What is it that would rock your world? Think about it now and write it down. Take a break from reading and do it.

8. *Visualize*: Once you get clarity about the bigger picture, your compelling vision, think about it and make it as real as possible, as tangible as possible. I want you to be able to imagine yourself in the future where you enjoy having

reached your vision. Can you see it? What do you smell? What do you hear? Who or what is around you? Make it like a short video clip in your mind. Do you have it? Make sure it is crystal-clear and hold on to it. Every day, start and end your day with this vision. This will be the fuel that will propel you forward. For this, you can also create a vision board, where you can put images of the life you envision. The result would be a photo-montage where you can actually see your compelling vision. Stick it in a place where you can see it more often. One look at it will be enough to revive your 'motivation' levels any time you need to.

Here is a short visualization activity for you to practise. Make yourself comfortable. Think of the activity you are procrastinating. Now, visualize yourself doing it and instead of dreading it or hating it, turn it into a best-case scenario. See yourself enjoying it. Make it as real as possible. Feel the deep positivity, witness how you enjoy yourself and then just see yourself finishing the activity. Experience the satisfaction at the end, the relief of completing the task; feel that fulfilling feeling.

Do this whenever you find yourself demotivated.

There will be days when you might not be able to give 100 per cent, but that's perfectly fine as long as you are consistent. Consistency is the key to mastery. Even if you take baby steps every day, you will end up experiencing massive success. So, develop the habit of taking small, digestible steps every day. And yes, take giant leaps on other days when you are super pumped, but never ever stop. Stay in action consistently.

Remember: Motivation follows action and mastery follows consistency.

By following the simple strategies discussed in this chapter, you can change your pain and pleasure associations for your greater good and learn the art of becoming a purposeful procrastinator.

'Only put off until tomorrow what you are willing to die having left undone.'

– Pablo Picasso

So, how do you feel now that you are more than half way through this incredible journey?

There is one very important aspect that keeps us from becoming 'masters' of our life, taking complete charge. If we could work on this area and change it, becoming our own master would be a cakewalk. We talk about this next.

14

CLAIM BACK YOUR POWER

How to be not stuck?

That colleague of mine always brings out the worst in me.

My boyfriend or girlfriend ruined my entire day.

My mother-in-law always manages to ruin my mood and makes me feel bad about myself.

My boss is my worst enemy; he makes me mad like no one else does.

Do any of the above statements sound familiar? If yes, then you have chosen to give away all your power to the world. You have given others the power to control how you feel, think, and act.

Some people are so affected by how others behave that they start to lose control of their life. They tend to hold grudges against people who have in some way hurt them or offended them. They often face difficulty setting healthy boundaries with people in their life and end up feeling angry towards these people for taking up their time and energy. They are easily offended by any negative feedback or criticism that comes their way.

These are people who have given away their peace of mind to the outside world. They allow people to dictate their life, be it their emotions or important decisions in their life. In other words, they have given the control of their lives to others.

Addiction to anything – food, shopping, drugs, sex, TV, technology, and so on – is also giving your power to things external to you. We allow these addictions to control our behaviour. The underlying belief is that we cannot be happy by ourselves, so we need these addictions to make us happy.

All the above behaviours demonstrate the characteristics of someone who has given all his or her power away to the world. How they feel and how they behave is all dictated by the outside world, be it people or circumstances. One of the worst outcomes of this behaviour is depression. Depression happens when we feel out of control in our lives. We feel we cannot change the world in order to create what we want, so we opt out of life to some degree. If we continue to stay in this depressed state, a state of helplessness, in extreme cases, it can lead to developing suicidal tendencies as well. Therefore, this is one area that certainly needs to be addressed.

The primary reason for all the above behaviours is lack of self-worth, self-acceptance, and self-approval. If you do not feel you are worthy of love and acceptance, you might find yourself tolerating unacceptable behaviours from other people. You are thus allowing the outside world's opinions to define who you are.

I have an old friend who is one such person. She is so volatile that if someone says something to her that she doesn't like, she starts yelling and arguing at the top of her voice, regardless of where she is or who the other person is. She cannot control this behaviour even when she is in public. She is a classic case of someone who has chosen to allow the outside world to control her feelings and behaviour. I call such people 'pseudo victims'.

If your boss or mother-in-law or colleague or spouse or friend makes you angry because they behave in a way that you don't approve of or they say things that you feel are hurtful and mean, you need to understand that none of these people are forcing you to feel that way. You always have the choice of feeling the way you want to feel.

When you give your power away to the world, you rob yourself of mental peace and lose sight of your life goals. It is very common for us to relinquish our power without realizing it. We exhibit this behaviour on a daily basis, which makes it a habit, which then starts reflecting in different areas of our life. Sometimes this habit takes a toll on our relationships, finances, business or health. It's a vicious loop of continuous disempowerment. This starts reflecting in our language and thoughts (self-talk to be precise), such as:

'My relationship is going for a toss.'

'My health is in a mess.'

'I never get what I want.'

'I don't think I can ever make enough money.'

These are the conversations that make us feel powerless. When we feel powerless, we end up creating more such situations that make us feel even more powerless.

Reena was a successful businesswoman. However, her biggest challenge were her personal relationships and her health. She had been married for seventeen years and had a teenage son and daughter. Her widowed mother-in-law too lived with her. Her husband was her partner in business as well. Their business was booming, but their personal relationships were not as what they would have wanted. Reena found her mother-in-law to be extremely annoying.

She felt that her mother-in-law, Bharti, was too controlling and kept undermining her authority on her children. Whatever rules Reena set for her children, she found Bharti encouraging the children to break them by saying things like, 'Even we have brought up children, but we never laid down such strict rules. Our children also used to eat junk and watch TV. And it never affected their studies. Look how well they have turned out in life.'

Bharti always criticized Reena for her parenting style, which made her resentful towards Bharti. Though on the outside, she would just smile and pretend that she was unaffected, she would be left seething with anger inside.

What made matters worse was that Reena was finding it difficult to maintain a good relationship with her two teenagers. It seemed that her children refused to listen to her. No matter what she told them to do, they would never do it and she would end up yelling and shouting at them. Reena blamed her mother-in-law for her children's rebellion. Whenever she shared her agony with her husband, he would say something like, 'Just ignore Ma. She's old. Trust me, she is a well-wisher,' or 'They are teenagers and their behaviour is just a reflection of their age.' Reena did not find solace in sharing her pain with her husband. She felt that he did not care for her and would never understand what she was going through. She had developed a lot of medical issues as well over the past five or six years; she had acid-reflux, anxiety, and high blood pressure. She was not in a healthy space.

When Reena spoke to me about her troubles, I asked her a few questions, just to make her aware that she herself had somewhere chosen to give her power away to her mother-in-law and children. She had handed over all her emotional and behavioural buttons to her children and Bharti. How she felt and behaved depended on these people in her life. And this constant stress was physically manifesting in her body in the form of a myriad medical issues.

Initially, she was reluctant to accept the fact that it was indeed she who was responsible for what was happening in her life. It is very easy to blame the outside world for your miseries, but it takes a lot of courage to take responsibility for them. Though it may seem like others are mean to you, the fact is that they are what they are because somewhere you have given them the power and the leeway to treat you that way. If you choose to become a doormat, how will people treat you? They will of course wipe their feet on you. Is that what you want?

When I asked her these questions, she realized for the first time that in fact it was she who had allowed this mess in her life. I asked her to reflect on how much time she spent every day thinking about Bharti and how her children didn't like her. Her answer was, 'I am literally thinking about these issues almost all the time, even when I am in the office. It keeps bothering me all the time.'

'And how does that affect your energy during the day?' I further enquired.

'Oh! Don't ask me that. I feel drained and tired all the time.'

'Do you want to continue feeling this way?'

'Of course not. That's why I am here talking to you,' she said.

I asked her to then get ready for some self-reflection. I made her go through some processes that helped her figure what was it about her that made her behave like a pseudo victim.

The very first insight she got was that she lacked self-worth, which makes one depend on others to feel good about themselves. You want everyone to like you, approve of you. The moment you see someone disapproving of you, you feel low. Why? Because you do not believe that you are worthy enough. Your self-worth depends on how others perceive you.

Secondly, she figured out that she was tolerating the toxic behaviour of the people around her because she had unconscious fears, leading to lack of confidence. She figured that she had a fear of losing control and fear of failure. She feared that she might fail as a mother and she feared that she might lose control to her mother-in-law. Also, since she had very low self-esteem, she believed that she was not good enough when it came to personal relations and ended up feeling helpless.

This realization helped Reena stand up for herself. I gave her a few exercises that would help her develop her self-esteem and confidence. I told her to be the same person at home that she was in her professional space – a strong and confident woman.

A few weeks later, when we met, I could see a positive shift in her. She told me that for the first time, she had gathered the courage to talk to her mother-in-law about what was troubling her and assertively set some ground rules. Initially, her mother-in-law was a little taken aback by her new avatar, but because she could see a new confidence in Reena, she complied. In a matter of a few months, Reena was able to create harmony in her relationships. Her children's behaviour towards her had softened and, of course, her relation with Bharti was improving as well. This is what Reena told me when we met after a few months:

'Rinku, what I have realized on this journey is that you lose your power when you fail to stand up for yourself. When you have this feeling in your body that tells you that you have been wronged and you do nothing about it. When you take shit from people and you know you shouldn't. That's what I was doing all these years. Having great personal relationships and perfect health were just dreams for me, which I thought were best left as dreams. I had given up all hope that these dreams would ever come true. I always had a self-conversation that I couldn't change because it wasn't in my hands. I was always playing my victim card, blaming, complaining and making excuses for all the things that were not working in my life. I was not ready to take responsibility for my life and kept on hoping that someday, someone would come and change my world. What I have finally realized and learnt is that I am the only one who can change my world; I am the master of my life. If I love myself enough, if I respect myself enough, if I believe in myself enough and if I choose to be fearless, I can create anything and everything that I want.'

Reena had now taken her power back from the world and was now totally in charge of her life. When I say 'power', I mean the ability to create desirable, positive changes in your life. It means to be in charge of your emotions and reactions. It means to understand and accept who you are, what you want, and never be apologetic about it. It means to face all your fears and render them powerless. Power is about knowing your worth enough to ask for what you want clearly and with confidence (like Reena did). Power is loving and valuing yourself enough, so that you don't need to seek outside approval. Power is not about intimidating others or using aggression to get what you want (what Reena was doing earlier with her children) – it never works.

Many people face similar challenges in their life. So, it is very important to understand how to take this power back from the world. Let's summarize the important steps that you need to take in order to gain back control of your life:

1. *Develop self-esteem and self-love*: Approve and love yourself for who you are. Believe that you are unique and special. You are not defined by other people's opinions. One of the simplest yet the most powerful exercises to develop self-love is the mirror exercise. Every time you look into the mirror, anywhere, say to the man or woman in the mirror, looking into his or her eyes, 'I love you. You are awesome. You are a rockstar.' You will be amazed how your self-esteem and self-worth will increase in a very short span. Make this a habit. If you can't speak it out aloud – for instance, when you are in a public space – just say these words to yourself in your mind.

2. *Become fearless*: Fears paralyze us. Don't let them overpower you. The only way to master fears is to face them. This will render them powerless and you will realize that you are much stronger than your fears.

3. *Learn to take responsibility*: When you take responsibility for everything in your life, be it success or failure, you will stop blaming the outside world for your problems, you will stop complaining about the things that are not working in your life and you will stop making excuses. You will realize that you are actually not a victim but a victor.

4. *Focus on what you want*: Instead of focusing on the behaviours of others, focus on yourself and examine what needs to change inside you. Learn to focus your energy

on things that you want. Focus on things that give you happiness. Just by shifting your focus, you will see how magically things will start to fall in place.

5. *Change your self-talk and watch your language*: Become conscious and aware of your negative self-chatter and the language you use on a daily basis and catch yourself whenever you indulge in it. This will help shift your language and self-talk to empowering and positive. (More details can be found in the chapter on language)

Always remember that you have the power to create what you want. All the power lies inside you. You are way more powerful than you ever imagined. By giving it away, you are depriving yourself of all your dreams. So, stand up and claim your power.

> ***'It's time to take your life back from the people who are causing you pain and making you unhappy. Remember this is your life and you are the author of your story. If you are stuck on the same page, just remember that at any moment you have the power to write a new chapter.'***
>
> ***– Anonymous***

The next chapter builds up on the things I shared in this one. To be able to claim your power back, you will need to learn the art of handling difficult people.

15

HOW TO HANDLE DIFFICULT PEOPLE

Ways to stabilize and improve difficult situations with grace

How do you define a difficult person?

A difficult person is someone who has certain emotional and behavioural traits that defy logic and make it difficult to communicate with them. Difficult people are everywhere. In fact, sometimes you too can be difficult. We all go through times when we don't act our best. However, some people are intrinsically difficult (I call them chronically difficult people); their behaviour is obnoxious and they are completely unaware of the negative impact they have on the people around them. Sometimes, they come across as people who derive pleasure from creating chaos and pushing other people's buttons.

We've all been there, trying to cope with such people. This person could be your boss, friend, colleague or a family member. The truth about chronically difficult people is that you cannot expect to reason with them. Trying to reason with an incredibly difficult person can lead to frustrating, maddening, and sometimes frightening situations, which ultimately causes a lot of stress.

Firstly, we need to understand the fact that when we are dealing with a difficult person, it is not about us, it's about them. So, never take anything that they say personally. Remember always that people who hurt are themselves hurt. They are fighting their own battles and their bad and difficult behaviour is a result of their mental and emotional state at the time. Some of these people could come across as angry, some could be always whining, some could be criticizing and finding fault with you, and some could be trying to pull you down or speaking ill of you. The fact is that all their behaviours come from deep-rooted insecurities that they have unconsciously developed over the years, leading to lack of self-esteem, belief, confidence, fear of rejection, and so on. These insecurities make these people behave the way they do, and the sad part is that they are not even aware of this. So, more than anything, view these people from a place of understanding and compassion.

Secondly, we need to understand that a person is not equal to their behaviour and that every behaviour arises from a good intention. Say, for example, you have a friend who is always complaining that you don't give her/him enough time and that you always ignore them, which you know is not the case. This behaviour ends up making you feel frustrated, angry, and drained. You don't look forward to meeting this friend anymore, because of their constant nagging and complaining.

Now what you need to see is the intent of their behaviour. The intent is that they love you and value you so much that they end up behaving as if they own you (which is not acceptable). So there is a conflict between their intention and their behaviour. In the case of normal people, their behaviour is in congruence with the intention, but not in the case of difficult people.

Now that we understand why difficult people behave the way they do, having this awareness will help you deal with them in a lot more effective manner. The first thing to consider is how difficult people affect you.

Researchers from the University of California, Berkeley, performed a series of experiments looking at the impact of chronic stress on the brain. They discovered that stress can have a lasting negative impact on the brain.[1] Exposure to even a few days of stress effects the neurons in the hippocampus – an important area in the brain responsible for memory, learning, and emotions. Weeks of stress cause reversible (temporary) damage to neuronal dendrites (the small 'arms' that brain cells use to communicate with each other), and months of stress can permanently destroy neurons. Stress is an alarming threat to your success. When stress gets out of control, your brain and your performance suffer along with your physical health. In fact, studies have revealed that stress is the number one factor that causes all diseases.

Recent research from the Department of Biological and Clinical Psychology at the Friedrich Schiller University in Germany found that exposure to stimuli that cause strong negative emotions – the same kind of exposure you get when dealing with difficult people – caused subjects' brains to have a massive stress response.[2] So, you can see that difficult people drive your brain into a stressed-out state that is extremely detrimental for you.

The truth is that these people do hurt you. It is often said, 'Your wound is probably not your fault, but your healing is your responsibility.' We are told to 'just learn to let go', which makes sense, but how do we actually let go of the pain and anger we feel towards such people? The answer is simple: By taking responsibility and accepting that it was you who allowed such people to treat you badly. This way, you take the power away from these people and take complete charge of your life.

Your second responsibility is to learn certain techniques, some coping and negotiation strategies, which can help you deal with these people. Here are a few of these effective techniques:

1. ***Develop self-love:*** Always believe that you deserve love and respect, and that no one can make you feel the way you don't want to feel. For this, you need to develop self-love. When I say self-love, I mean to become your best friend. How does your best friend treat you? How much can you count on your best friend? Do you do the same with your own self? Ask yourself these questions and start with changing any self-talk that makes you feel lesser and victimized. Stop telling yourself that 'you are not good enough', 'you deserve to be treated like this', and all self-talk that drains you. For at least thirty days, consciously catch yourself when you talk meanly to yourself. The moment you catch

yourself doing so, write down these negative statements. Now flip them and write the opposite statements – positive ones. Always carry a small writing pad or a notebook with you to complete this exercise. Negative self-talk is unrealistic, unnecessary and self-defeating. It sends you into a downward emotional spiral from which it is difficult to pull out. You should avoid negative self-talk at all costs.

2. ***Ignore the behaviour:*** We already know now that a person is not his/her behaviour. So when you encounter a difficult person, ignore the behaviour that you don't like. One of my friends belongs to the chronically difficult people category. He has a habit of complaining that I ignore him, that I don't have time for him, that I have changed so much and so on. Recently, we met to catch up with a group of friends, where his behaviour was extremely obnoxious and I could see how he was trying to pull me down and make me feel bad and angry. He tried his best to elicit a reaction from me. Though I did feel bad about his behaviour, I chose to ignore that part of his behaviour and lead the conversation in a different direction. Not once in the entire evening did he succeed in making me feel angry or guilty. Why? Because my conscience was clear and moreover, I love myself and know that it is my responsibility to protect myself from such emotional attacks. Since he could not get to me, the next morning, he messaged me blaming me and making me feel angry or guilty. How I handled this brings us to the next step.

3. ***Wait. Let the emotion die a natural death*:** Every emotion has a duration for which it lasts. There is no emotion that lasts forever. So, when my friend was writing all those annoying messages to me, I chose not to check his messages, because whenever someone is charged with an emotion, especially a negative emotion, their rational mind does not function. So it is best not to respond then and instead wait. I did not respond that day and called him the next day. I spoke normally, as if his outburst had had no impact on me. This gave him the signal that I was unaffected by his obnoxious behaviour and that I was not interested in having any conversation around such matters. Also, since it was a new day, he was not as emotionally charged as he was the day before. The conversation that I had with him on the phone brings us to our next step.

4. ***Forgive, but never forget*:** When we encounter toxic people who could sometimes be an integral part of our lives, such as a family member, it becomes all the more important to learn the art of forgiving. You need to forgive the toxic person, not because they deserve it, but because you deserve peace and happiness. Holding on to resentment and anger is like holding a burning coal in your hand; it burns you, not the toxic person. And you don't deserve that pain. Forgiveness starts with self-love, along with the understanding that the other person is fighting his/her own battle; their behaviour is more about them and not about you. Emotionally intelligent people are quick to forgive, but that doesn't

mean that they *forget*. Forgiveness requires letting go of what's happened so that you can move on, but it doesn't mean you'll give the wrongdoer another chance to repeat their behaviour. So don't forget that these people have a tendency to hurt you. Be on guard when around them and be assertive enough not to allow them the opportunity to hurt you again. That's why it is important never to forget. So, going back to my conversation with my friend – before I called him, I had forgiven him already, which placed the control of the situation entirely in my hand. Because I could forgive him, I had the emotional strength to get the outcome that I wanted out of this situation.

5. ***Be Assertive***: When I did not talk about his bad behaviour and the obnoxious messages he had sent a day before, he was surprised. He started the subject again. The moment he entered the obnoxious mode again (which they will do in most cases) and started talking in a tone that I did not like, I said 'I appreciate that you can share your thoughts and feelings with me, but I do not like anyone talking to me like that. Also, I don't believe in having to give regular proofs of friendship to you or anyone. If you doubt my intentions as a friend, then I'm sorry, I choose to quit. This is not my definition of friendship.' There was a silence of shocked disbelief. Since that conversation, he has not misbehaved with me till today. *Assertiveness*. Sometimes, the toxic person becomes so irrational and unstoppable that no strategy seems to work. That is when you need to

step out, speak up for yourself, stand in your power and be assertive. The moment you do that, either the annoying behaviour will change (as in my case) or the person will exit from your life. In either case, it's a win-win for you.

6. ***Draw healthy boundaries:*** Step 4 was about not forgetting the toxic person's behaviour, because they always have the tendency to repeat their behaviour (unless they choose to do something about it). Therefore, it is essential to draw healthy boundaries with these people. For example, if it's a work colleague, you can choose not to interact with them at a personal level, limiting your interaction only to work. Limit your time with them; if you must interact, keep things short by excusing yourself from the conversation or bringing a third party into the conversation. If that does not work, follow the next step.

7. ***Stop listening to them:*** A good listener is someone who is superb at building rapport, which is generally through eye contact and body language. When you are obliged to interact with a toxic person, the opposite strategy works best. You break the rapport. Don't maintain eye contact, keep checking you mobile and appear disinterested in them. This will send a strong signal to them and they will eventually stop bothering you.

8. ***Acceptance:*** Accept that this person will never become the friend, colleague, or sibling you want. The sooner you accept this, the better it will be for you.

9. ***Calm down and vent out the negativity:*** Finally, all the emotional trauma that you go through while dealing with such people can take a toll on you, so it is very important to vent any negative emotion that you are left with; let it all out. There are many ways you can do that – you can go for a run, exercise in the gym, catch up with happy and inspiring friends, go shopping and, if you feel overwhelmed and want to scream and cry, I recommend that you do so. Go to your room, lock it and scream or cry out loud. The only condition is that you finish this exercise within ten minutes – not a second more than that.

Sometimes, if everything you've tried fails to change their behaviour towards you, it is time to tell them that your relationship with them is not working. You don't have to feel guilty. First, try setting boundaries. Limit interactions and try to take their words less seriously. If that doesn't work and all the above strategies don't help, you might have to cut this person out of your life entirely. At the end of the day, it's your life and you are the decision-maker.

> ***'Don't waste another minute dealing with a toxic, negative, energy-draining person ... They love being argumentative, combative and abusive. Run for your life as quickly as possible.'***
>
> *– Les Brown*

So, here we are, ready to dive into the last idea in the 'Take Charge' section. If you can learn and internalize this one idea, it will keep you in a perpetual state of bliss.

16

THE ART OF LIVING IN THE MOMENT

Let go of the past, don't fear the future.

Do you have sleepless nights thinking about unpleasant things that happened in the past? It could be anything, from a bad relationship or suffering a financial loss to making a terrible mistake or saying something you regret or any traumatic experience you have been through.

Do you constantly keep worrying about how things will turn out in your future, be it your career, health or well-being of you and your loved ones, or your future financial security?

If your answer to the above questions is a 'Yes', then welcome to the 'D and W Club', where D stands for 'dwelling in the past' and W stands for 'worrying about the future'. A lot of people belong to this club, not because there is anything wrong with them but because this is human nature. As humans, our basic instinct is survival. That's the reason we find ourselves worrying so much and fearing so many things. Most of the time all these worries and fears are unfounded and baseless, because the fact, in this modern age, is that there is no real threat to our survival. But because of the way we are designed, we start imagining things that might go wrong in the future, or remembering unpleasant things that have happened in the past. That makes us fear that they might happen again.

Let's dive into the first part, *dwelling in the past*. Why do the majority of us have the habit of holding on to the past?

Rita was a highly successful and smart entrepreneur in her early thirties. She was any man's dream. But Rita was averse to the idea of having a romantic relationship, let alone getting married. It was not that she had never fallen in love or had a relationship before, but her first love, which had culminated into marriage, had turned into a nightmare. She had only been twenty-one when she discovered that her husband was nothing like what he had been before they got married – a loving and caring boyfriend. He was short-tempered and would pick fights even on small things, such as changing the temperature of the air conditioner. Initially, Rita thought that perhaps it was a temporary phase and he had some issues at his workplace. But to her horror, this behaviour became worse with time. The first time he hit her, came as a shock to her. How could someone who loved her so dearly harm her?

She still had hope and tried to convince him to see a psychologist. The day she raised this subject became the worst day of her life. This suggestion made him so angry that he lost all sense of humanity. He had beaten her and brutally raped her that she was left with a broken arm and fractured ribs. He did not even bother to call a doctor and left her bleeding on the floor. She had to crawl to get to her mobile and call the ambulance.

It took her almost six months to recover. Though her physical wounds healed, the scar left on her soul seemed permanent. While she was in the hospital, she made an important decision – to end her marriage with the beast. It took her more than a year to get divorced. It was a long and ugly battle, where he stooped to the lowest levels possible, accusing her of promiscuity and immorality. All of this left her deeply hurt and scarred within.

After her divorce, she decided to gather herself and do what she had always dreamt of doing: her long-cherished dream of starting her own business. This also seemed like the best way for her to heal emotionally. She immersed herself completely in creating her own business, which she did successfully. Along the way, she got many proposals for marriage, but she was absolutely against getting married again. She did not even want a relationship. She feared that what she had experienced earlier might happen again and also, she had lost faith in love. She kept telling herself, 'I am better off without a man in my life. I don't need love.'

Rita is not alone. There are many people who are in the same situation as Rita's, holding on to something that happened in the past and unwilling to move forward. This was an extreme case, but we have the inclination to keep ruminating about past events, especially unpleasant ones. It could be anything – an argument with your spouse, a presentation gone wrong in office, someone insulting you in front of other people, and so on. Some people are more prone to dwelling on the past than others. Nearly everyone dwells on the past at some point, but some people do it more often. These are people who get stuck in the past.

So, why do we stay anchored in the past?

The number one reason why we stay anchored in the past is the impact of our negative and bad experiences. When we go through a bad experience, it lingers, either in the form of shame, anger, or guilt. There is an intense emotion attached to it. We feel like a victim and start believing that we don't deserve happiness. This eventually develops into a fear of moving on, like in Rita's case. She feared that her past would repeat, so she refrained from giving love another chance.

Another situation in which people stay stuck in the past is when their present circumstances are not favourable. Often I hear people talking about 'the good old days'. Why is that? It is because they want to stay distracted from the present realities and challenges, and the best way is to keep harping on their past laurels.

Chitra, a friend, had been a 'beauty queen' in her college days. She had the perfect figure, the best features, lovely hair and skin. She was every girl's envy and every boy's dream. When I met her a couple of years back, I was shocked to see an obese woman with no glow on her face. Throughout our conversation, she kept on talking about the 'good old days.' Her conversation was all about: 'Remember when I was crowned the beauty queen in college?' and related events. I could see how she had kept herself anchored to her past glory because the current reality was just the opposite.

This also happens in cases opposite to that of Rita: people who are unhappy in their current relationships tend to spend a lot of time thinking about a past love. They might have thoughts such as 'If I had married my first love, life would have been better.' When you dwell on good memories, it can also cause you to lose connection with the present. You will find yourself romanticizing the past or longing for things to be the way they were, instead of focusing on improving your present. This attitude of feeding yourself thoughts that your past was better than your present can actually take away all your present happiness. It stops you from taking action and doing something to change your current reality, like in Chitra's case.

Staying stuck in the past while the rest of the world changes and moves forward is not helpful and is emotionally unhealthy. People who stay stuck in the past have no idea that this can lead to clinical depression, affect our decision-making skills and also to many diseases. If you keep ruminating about negative events in the past, you will keep feeling negative emotions and when the emotions are negative, the brain has a tendency to trigger more negative memories to validate the current emotional state. This is a vicious cycle and it eventually leads to a range of emotional distresses and physical illnesses.

We miss out on living in the present and enjoying life to its fullest. The truth is, what has happened is in the past. Good or bad, it will never come back again. So if there are bad memories in the past, let's look at learning from those experiences, take the lessons and move on; if they are good memories, then cherish them and see how you can create more good memories in your present, because our present is all we have control over.

Here are some of the ways in which you can break the habit of ruminating in the past:

1. ***Let the emotions flow:*** One of the tendencies we have is to hold back our emotions. We have been taught not to express our emotions, which is extremely unhealthy. Ignoring our emotions is the biggest mistake to make. To remove the anchor from the past and move forward, feel the emotions and see what exactly you are feeling. It could be a mix of more than one emotion, which is fine. Ask yourself: *What emotions do I feel now when I revisit that experience?* Write what you feel and where you physically feel those emotions in your body. Then, if you feel like you need to cry or shout to let out any anger or sadness or hurt, just do it. Let the

tears come until you can cry no more; scream out, shout into the mirror until the frustration diminishes.

2. ***Shift your focus:*** Whenever you catch yourself thinking about your past, shift your focus. Think about good things happening right now. Don't say that there are no good things in your life right now; just look around and you will find them. It could be your little kid, your best friend, your spouse, your beautiful house, the park near you, the flowers in the garden, the gentle breeze. Or just think about a place you feel nurtured in, your favourite foods, or read your favourite book – anything that leaves a smile on your face; focus on that.

3. ***Practise forgiveness:*** I keep repeating this because this is one of the most powerful ways to 'take charge' of your life. However, this is something most people are reluctant to do initially. The last thing we ever want to do is to forgive the people who hurt us. Some people think, *Why should I forgive someone who has caused me so much pain?* But forgiveness does not mean what that person did was right or that you deserved it; it is about giving you a chance to heal and move on. So many people live while holding on to past occurrences that hinder them from reaching their highest potential. You really can't move forward and embrace anything new while you still are holding on to old issues, old regrets, old shame, anger or guilt.

Although you think you are punishing the other person, the reality is that you actually are hurting and punishing yourself. True forgiveness isn't about other people and their actions; it is about you. In fact, it has absolutely nothing to do with how or why you felt wronged. It's simply a process of releasing any resentment or painful feelings towards yourself or someone else. Forgive yourself also, if you feel guilty about something, instead of beating yourself up for your past mistakes. Understand that no one is perfect and we all make mistakes.

4. ***Take the lessons and learning:*** Instead of dwelling on the past, take time out to reflect on the experience and look at it in a way that it will benefit you in your present. For example, in Rita's case, had she chosen to take the right lessons from her experience she wouldn't have developed limiting beliefs about love. For this, ask questions, such as:
   - What actually happened? Write about the facts, not the emotion. Revisit the experience, but with the intention of not focusing on how you felt then, but what really happened. This will help separate the emotion from the experience and when there is no emotion, the tendency of dwelling on it declines.
   - How has this experience changed me as a person? This might not necessarily be a bad change the way Rita might perceive: 'It made me bitter about love.' Think of how this experience made you better and stronger. Perhaps you

learned to stand up and speak for yourself, you became more assertive, you learnt to take your own decisions, or perhaps you learnt to be more honest. Trust me, some of the best life lessons can be learnt from the most challenging and darkest times that you have endured.

- o How can I use this to empower myself? Now this is the best one. This will help you create a future that you would have otherwise thought impossible. Like in Rita's case. Not all her takeaways from her negative experience were negative. She ended up starting her own business and succeeding in it too. Who would have imagined that a woman whose only dream was to become a good wife and a mother would one day become a successful entrepreneur? Where did all this power come from? From her negative experience. So ask this question and you never know what might come up for you.

5. ***Take responsibility***: Again, I keep repeating this, because it's the key to taking control of your life. Repeating is the best way to internalize things. Responsibility means to take charge of your life and stop pointing fingers at others. Instead of blaming people or situations for your past pains, tell yourself that 'I take complete responsibility for what happened and I choose to move forward taking all the lessons from this experience.'

Taking responsibility does not mean that you start putting the blame on yourself; it means acknowledging the past from a place of compassion for yourself and choosing to move forward. When we blame and complain, we give our power away and make ourselves small. So make sure you are not in the blaming–complaining zone.

Let us now move on to the second part, which is *worrying about the future*. Sheena is my a client and she is in her mid-50s. She was a branch manager in a public sector bank, would soon retire. Whenever I had a conversation with her, she would talk about how she was worried about her retirement and how would she manage life after: 'I am so worried about how my life will be after my retirement. What will I do, sitting at home? I don't want to be dependent on my children. Oh God! What if my children send me to an old age home?' She was constantly worried about her future.

Me: You know what you are doing, Sheena? You are thinking ahead, trying to predict what will happen in your future. Can anyone really predict the future?

Sheena: No, we can't predict the future, but in all likelihood this is what will happen.

Me: Are you sure this will happen?

Sheena: Um ... not really.

Me: See, instead of being in the present and enjoying what you are doing in the moment, you are getting anxious about something that is non-existent.

Sheena: Then how do I get rid of this anxiety? Thinking about the future makes me distressed.

This is the question that I shall address now. A majority of people have a habit of worrying about the future. It could be anything from worrying about the economy collapsing or your boss firing you to worrying about possibly getting dumped or worrying about the well-being of your loved ones. This worry is natural, because the future is all about uncertainty, and somewhere inside, we are all uncomfortable about uncertainty.

The fear of the unknown is one of the primary fears. However, if we fixate on the unknown, we will eventually start telling ourselves stories that are not true. We need to understand that consistent worrying has both short-term and long-term effects on our well-being, just like dwelling in the past. Worrying is a behaviour that steals our joy, affects our sleep patterns and our decision-making. Whenever we face new situations, it is normal to feel overwhelmed, but worrying about the unknown does not serve us in any way. It is, in fact, futile. Latest research shows that worrying has several physiological effects:

- Constant worrying causes stress, which physically and emotionally drains you. Plus, it has now been proven that stress is the number-one killer; the root of all diseases.
- It hampers your focus.
- It decreases your creativity and your rational thinking.

- It affects your sleep.
- It clouds your decision-making capabilities.

So, what do you say? Is worrying worth it? The best way to rid yourself of this life-threatening habit is to follow these simple ideas:

1. ***Change your focus:*** I keep talking about focus, because this is one of the most powerful tools that help create a change. Focus on the things that you love and enjoy. Instead of focusing on the future, something that is far off in the distance, focus on things that are right in front of you that you might be overlooking. Ask yourself this powerful question: *What is right in front of me that I am not looking at?*

2. ***Surround yourself with positive people:*** Seek out positive and inspiring people and communities and distance yourself from the ones that encourage your worrying habit.

3. ***Master your emotions.***

4. ***Develop the habit of planning:*** People who suffer from extreme worrying about the unknown should develop the habit of creating a plan of action. For example, people worry about their finances would benefit immensely from financial planning, which would take care of their budgeting and savings. This would take a lot of their anxiety away.

5. *Have faith:* Trust is the opposite of worry. When you trust the higher power that has created you and your world, things are automatically taken care of.

Dwelling on the past or worrying about the future can make you lose sight of your present. Learn to live in the moment and trust the process of life. Every moment in the present is creating our future and every moment passing by is becoming our past. So, from now on, if you want your past and future filled with happiness, learn to live in the now. It's an art.

> ***'What matters is to live in the present, live now, for every moment is now. It is your thoughts and acts of the moment that create your future. The outline of your future path already exists, for you created its pattern by your past.'***
>
> ***– Shirdi Sai Baba***

Let us now explore the last section, Food for Thought. I call the ideas shared in this section catalysts; just like a catalyst increases the rate of a chemical reaction, these ideas will hasten the speed of your progress and transformation.

III

FOOD FOR THOUGHT

17

DO YOU HAVE AN IDEATION ZONE?

Ideas, like plants, need a place to grow.

Did you know that, every day, every person gets at least one great idea – an idea that, if implemented, can change lives?

Newton discovered gravity when an apple fell from a tree; he had the thought that there has to be something that makes everything fall. The chair that we are sitting on was once just an idea. The house that we are living in was once just an idea. Ideas are the roots from which all discoveries, inventions, and businesses have emerged. The foundation of all progress – political, technological, economical, educational, any kind at all – is ideas. No innovation is possible without ideas.

However, when it comes to sharing ideas, most people hesitate. There are many reasons for this behaviour, right from the fear of ridicule and rejection to the fear of their ideas being stolen or them not receiving any credit if the idea proves to be a success. This attitude of holding on to one's knowledge is detrimental to one's growth and evolution. If you want to grow and become better at what you do, developing the habit of sharing your ideas is the fastest way to achieve it.

One of the factors that is common amongst individuals and organizations that are doing really well is the sharing of ideas, which is also called brainstorming. A lot has been written about how sharing ideas at the workplace would help create better solutions, help everyone improve together, and quickly reach higher levels of expertise. All of this is indeed true and worth following.

However, this chapter is more about how ideas can help us create the life we want, how developing a regular habit of sharing our thoughts can lead to major breakthroughs in our lives.

I want to share a personal experience here. For as long as I have been married, my husband and I have had a habit of going for long walks after dinner. During these walks, we end up talking about how our respective days went and share our thoughts and feelings about almost everything. This habit has served us quite well; not only did it help strengthen our bond but also has led to us beginning to understand each other better. It has helped us both in our personal lives as well as in our careers.

I quite vividly remember the day – a couple of years back – when I was going through a professional challenge. It was something so grave that I was almost on the verge of giving up. Needless to say, I was not in a good state emotionally. Everything seemed to be falling apart. However, the after-dinner walk being an almost religious tradition for us, we went for it.

We took the same route; the usual walking track in the park near our house. The moment we stepped on the track and started talking, ideas started flooding our minds, as always. We discussed them at length while walking and, to my surprise, I found clarity about what I needed to do.

On our way back, I realized that whenever we took our after-dinner walks, we ended up getting great insights and solutions to so many of our problems; but we had never realized this before. I shared this insight with my husband, and he agreed completely. I got over that challenge by implementing the idea we got that night.

This was a major breakthrough in my life. I had discovered something extremely powerful and profound. I did have an idea about why we got such insights only during our after-dinner walks. I wanted to confirm something else as well. So, one night, I told my husband that instead of walking in the park, we should walk within our block only, to which he agreed. That night, though we shared everything as usual, we did not have any great insights and felt something was amiss. The second day, I told him to skip the walk and, instead, sit at home and talk. He agreed rather reluctantly, and we ended up watching TV instead of sharing. I got my answer. I shared my insight with my husband the next day.

'Have you noticed that whenever we go for our after-dinner stroll in the park, we have great insights and ideas? We have gotten solutions to so many of our professional and personal problems there, isn't it?' I asked him.

'Hmm... I never really realized this. I guess you're right,' he said, smiling.

'The reason I insisted on taking the walk in our block day before yesterday and on sitting at home last night was that I wanted to confirm whether it had anything to do with the place.'

'What do you mean?' He was now curious.

'I mean, the walkway in the park is like an anchor for us. The moment we start walking there, great ideas start flowing in our minds. I didn't realize this all these years, but the other day, when we found the solution to my biggest challenge ever, it got me thinking about this. When we chose another place to walk, or sat at home, there were no great ideas. In fact, when we chose to sit at home, we ended up watching TV, which we don't even like! Didn't you notice this?'

'Oh my god! Yes, you're right! This is amazing!' He was all smiles.

'Let's call that place our "Ideation Zone"', I suggested.

From that day onwards, that walking track in the park became our 'Ideation Zone', where we got solutions to our problems. This zone was our anchor. An anchor is an external or internal trigger with which a specific internal response is associated. So, to invoke the same response, all we need to do is invoke the trigger. The trigger could be a word, sentence or thought (internal) or anything external like pressing your thumb or patting your shoulder or a place, like in our case.

We had unknowingly created an anchor where our brain got the signal for the creative juices to start flowing. Initially, all this happened without our awareness, but now that we knew, we started making the most of it. The title of this book, *My Life I Decide,* which is also the title of my signature workshop, was a result of our interactions in our 'Ideation Zone'.

A few years later, we shifted to a new house, which had a beautiful terrace. Now there was no way to walk in the old park, so we created a new anchor. The terrace was now our new 'Ideation Zone'. I then also created an 'Ideation Zone' in my workplace, where my team and I sat and came up with great ideas.

I highly recommend creating ideation zones, both in our homes and workplaces. The question now is, *how does one create an ideation zone?*

There are two important things that you need to do:

- ***Who you ideate with is important:*** Firstly, it's very important to identify the people or person with whom you share your thoughts. I call them my Ideation Buddies. This person has to ideally be your close acquaintance, someone who has similar dreams and intentions, and most importantly, someone who respects you and your knowledge. This makes the process of ideation fruitful. If you want to create an ideation zone in your workplace, choose a team comprising of people who are inspiring, driven, and open to sharing. Otherwise, you will not be able to create an anchor that helps trigger the creative part of your brains.

Don't be hesitant to include people who always seem to have a contrary viewpoint as long as they respect you and are open to listening. In fact, no single person can have the perfect idea. When we have more people, we end up getting different perspectives to the same problem; a single person would be limited to just a single viewpoint. Every person is different and sees things differently, which helps get a 360-degree view of the situation and exposes you to sides you had never thought of before. Make sure you are not ideating with people who are trying to pull you down or people whose intentions are not good.

- ***Where you ideate is important:*** Secondly, the place you choose has to be appealing. It should be a place that evokes highly positive feelings inside you and where you love spending time. For instance, when we shifted to this new house, the first thing I did was to identify the ideation zone. I looked for a place that would evoke the most positive feelings. When I went up and saw the terrace, I loved it and knew instantly that this was my new ideation zone. Now we come to our terrace for the after dinner walks. In the office scenario, if you feel there is no place like this, you can create one by decorating and designing it in a way that is pleasing and pleasant.

Remember, ideas are not permanent. They come and go, so it's a great habit to keep a small booklet, which I call my Ideation Booklet, and a pen handy, so you can write them down the moment you get an idea and later discuss in the ideation zone with your ideation buddies. Be open to ideas always, no matter when they appear, where they come from, or how stupid they might seem. The moment you come across one, just write it down.

Also, develop the art of listening. Instead of just focusing on sharing your thoughts with your ideation buddies, focus on listening to their ideas too. Don't interject when others are sharing; listen to them with an open mind. When you do this, you will realize that you gain a lot more insights and build on your existing knowledge.

So, are you ready to create your ideation zone?

> ***'Great minds discuss ideas; average minds discuss events; small minds discuss people.'***
>
> ***– Eleanor Roosevelt***

Next in the Food for Thought section, we will explore how we can utilize our pains, challenges and failures to become the person who has the power to create magic in her/his life.

18

ARE YOU MAKING THE MOST OF YOUR DIPS?

Every time you sink low is an opportunity to rise higher than before.

Recently, I saw actor Sanjay Dutt's interview on a TV show. Before this interview, all I knew about him was that he had had an intense struggle with drugs during the earlier part of his life and later served a 42-months sentence for possessing weapons supplied by gangsters during the 1993 Mumbai bomb blasts. Besides this, he had a tumultuous personal life, which ended with him finally marrying his present wife in what happens to be his third marriage.

But, for the first time, I saw the real person, and the strength of character that he possesses left me awestruck. One thing that stood out was how he made the best of all these harsh situations.

He first spoke about his long ordeal with drugs that lasted twelve years. He said he had done every kind of drug on this planet. He narrated an incident when he once saw a mosquito trying to bite his arm and falling dead; such was the extent of damage the drugs had done to his body.[1]

He decided that come what may, no matter what the physical pain he has to endure, he would get himself out of the addiction, and he did. Today he inspires the youth to never get into drugs and to love their life, love their work, love their family; all these are blessings and any day better than drugs. He shared how the most difficult part starts after rehab, when there is a strong temptation to relapse. That's when one needs one's willpower the most.

Then he shared his experience in jail. When he found himself in jail and knew there was no way he could escape it, he told himself, *Okay, so whatever has happened has happened. I will not keep cribbing about why all this happened to me, as that is not going to help me. What is it that will help me now? How can I make the most of this situation?* That's when he decided that he would start working at losing weight and getting fitter. He did not have access to a gym or a personal trainer inside the jail, but that did not deter him. He started running in the yard, lifting big buckets of water, using the clotheslines to work out. He learnt to make paper bags and read holy texts, such as the Bhagavad Geeta, Ramayana, Shiv and Ganesh Puranas, Bible, Quran Sharif and Guru Granth Sahib. Besides that, he taught himself Marathi.

He also worked as a radio jockey and in the *natak mandali* (theatre group) in jail, where he taught some sixty to seventy convicts serving out life sentences to act, dance, and express themselves through skits and small plays. This exercise culminated in a cultural function held after six months of practice, to which senior jail authorities as well as filmmaker Rajkumar Hirani were invited. Sanjay came out a winner in almost all the dips life threw at him.

He decided that instead of acting like a victim he would utilize his time to learn and do things, which he would have never done had he not gone through these dips. The person who came out of all these dips was a much better version of the person who he was earlier. His journey is inspiring as it teaches us how to evolve from our dips.

Life is a series of events, sometimes good, sometimes painfully bad. These ups and downs, joys and sorrows, successes and failures are a part of life. One day, everything seems great in your life and then something happens. It could be losing a loved one, a job, your health, your home, or all your savings. Whenever we encounter such dips in our life, we feel like we did not deserve it and that life is not fair. Such unexpected dips tend to leave us frustrated and angry. We do not have any control over these situations, but what we can control is how we deal with them.

When something bad happens, some people choose to feel victimized. They look for something or someone outside them to blame. They keep looking for reasons and mistakes that led to the dip, without realizing that this attitude will make things worse and leave them feeling more miserable.

However, mentally strong people like Sanjay Dutt choose to take responsibility of the situation, make the most of it, and move on. This is the best way to deal with difficult situations, because this improves the chances of emerging from it faster.

> ***'Life is 10 per cent what happens to you and 90 per cent how you respond to it.'***
>
> ***– Charles R. Swindoll***

How we choose to respond to negative situations in life is what determines how quickly we can get over them and move on. What we need to understand is that difficulties will be present throughout our life at different stages and ages; there is no running away from them. Difficult times come to test our spirit. We all have unlimited reserves of inner strength and resilience that help us cope with whatever life throws at us. Difficult times come in our lives to help us unleash this tremendous strength. For example, in Sanjay Dutt's case, had he allowed fear, worry, regret, unhappiness or disappointment to take control of him, he would have never discovered his coping skills and inner strength. The fact that he chose to deal with his situation instead of playing victim helped him discover many hidden talents and abilities within him. We all have control over how we choose to react and act.

Dealing with a bad and difficult situation is similar to dealing with grief. People go through the same stages when they face these dips as when they go through grief: denial, anger, bargaining, depression and, finally, acceptance. In a nutshell, when we are going through a dip, we feel an amalgamation of strong emotions, which is very normal. Emotions are nature's way of dealing with situations, so do not ignore these emotions. Do not try to suppress these emotions. They have a natural time span and will eventually die.

However, for some people, it takes more time than others, and in worse cases, this period goes on for too long. This is when people experience depression or become suicidal. In such cases, one must seek medical help.

We cannot fight our emotions, but we can choose to accept what's happened, regardless of how we feel about it. *Acceptance* is the first step towards learning to deal with your dips in a constructive way. The sooner you accept, the sooner you can take some action, like Sanjay (exercising, reading and writing and other things). Taking *constructive action* is the only way to change how you feel.

Another important factor that can help us make the most of our dips is *what* we choose to *focus* on. The natural reaction to an unpleasant situation is 'life is not fair', but this belief will make matters worse. Nothing in life is fair or unfair. Everything is what we make of it. Yes, kindness should be reciprocated;

hard work should be rewarded, but is that always possible? People will not always behave the way we want them to and things will not always work out the way we want them to. So, instead of feeling angry at the world and bad for ourselves, we should focus on healing and construction. This shift in focus is a very powerful way of emerging as stronger, wiser, and better.

Difficult times teach us many more lessons than good times. These are invaluable lessons that help us deal with future difficulties with a lot more ease and patience. The dips in our lives exist to teach us certain important life lessons that shape our lives. So, whenever you go through a dip ask yourself,

- *What is life trying to teach me from this experience?*
- *If I emerge a winner on the other side of this crisis, will I be a better version of me?*

This *self-enquiry* will illuminate profound life lessons, which will in turn help you create the life that you want. Self-enquiry is also a powerful way to realize that the problem that seems so challenging might actually not be as catastrophic as we are making it out to be in our minds. Most situations are not as horrible as they appear to be and can be solved. Ask yourself:

- *Is this situation really the end of the world for me?*
- *What if I end up with a better solution (a better job, a better relationship, better health, etc.) on the other side of this situation?*

Vaibhav was a top-shot senior executive in a corporate business for over two decades. One day, out of the blue, he found himself jobless. Though he received an excellent severance package, this rejection completely shattered him. After all, he had given his prime years to this industry and helped them make millions. This seemed like the end of the world for Vaibhav. He now had a choice, to either feel and behave like a victim and make matters even worse, or make the most of this dip. Fortunately, he chose the latter. Though he was emotionally a wreck, he chose to accept this fact. He then chose to take constructive action. His focus was on healing and construction.

He entered the self-enquiry mode and asked himself all the questions listed above. Here they are again, to help you remember them:

- *What is life trying to teach me from this experience?*
- *If I emerge a winner on the other side of this crisis, would I be a better version of me?*
- *Is this situation really the end of the world for me?*
- *What if I end up with a better solution on the other side of this situation?*

This helped him start afresh. He first decided to go on a month long vacation with his family to Europe. This had been his wife's and his dream for years. So, he took this as an opportunity to spend quality time with his family and explore Europe.

While on vacation, he had many constructive discussions with his wife. During their discussions, he realized that maybe this was an opportunity for him and his wife to start their own business together, something they had been avoiding for so many years, for the fear of failure and financial insecurity.

But now, since he had no job, there was nothing to lose – perhaps this was life's way of pushing him towards his real calling. After they returned from a fantastic vacation, they started exploring different business ideas and consulting business coaches. Finally, they found what they were looking for. They decided to get funding for their idea. So they started working on developing a bulletproof business plan and meeting investors. After every initial rejection, they would sit and figure out the missing piece and further improve their pitch. After a long wait and after going through much rejection, failure, and pain, they got an investor who was completely impressed by their idea. This was the beginning of a new chapter in their lives and they were eventually able to build their own business empire. All this could happen because Vaibhav decided to see his dips as opportunities to create something new. His consistent action and resilience finally helped him get to where he wanted.

Now, had Vaibhav not been fired from his job, do you think he would have even thought of starting his own business, let alone actually doing it?

These dips are blessings in disguise and they come to push us on the path to creating an extraordinary life.

'Victory is always possible for the person who refuses to stop fighting.'

– Napoleon Hill

We are almost at the end of our journey. There is one more very important idea that I need to share with you. This is the last idea of our Food for Thought part as well as the last idea of this book. It may be the last, but it's not the end. In fact, I have saved the best for the last.

19

THE MISSING PIECE

Strength for the journey ahead

Q: What do you want from your life?

A: I want plenty of money in my bank account, so that I can have access to everything that I desire.

Sounds familiar? I bet it does.

Most of us end up chasing money because the external world has told us that money is the only ingredient that's important to lead a secure and successful life. If you have enough financial security, then you will be happy forever – that's the common belief. Therefore, most of us end up believing that money is our ultimate goal. Then why is it that most of us are either unable to make loads of money or even if we do, we end up feeling empty?

Bronnie Ware, an Australian nurse and counsellor, worked many years taking care of terminally ill people. Most of them had less than twelve weeks to live. As part of the therapy, Bronnie would ask them if they had any regrets in their lives. The one answer that stood out and was common to most of them was that they regretted not the things they had done but the things they did not do, the risks they never took, the dreams they didn't pursue.

Think about it. What would you regret the most when you are lying on your deathbed?

We need to understand that life is not meant for simply going to work, waiting for the weekend, and paying your rents and bills. Every single person on this planet is unique and is born with a *gift*. The sole purpose of our being is to discover that gift and share it with the world. This special gift comes wrapped in a box called Dreams. The dreams that we are scared will never become reality, the dreams that we wish could come true but are hesitant to pursue. It's this fear of following our dreams that creates an emptiness in our lives. When we keep doing everything except the 'One' important thing that we were born to do, we feel unfulfilled.

When I ask people 'What is life?', the most common response is: *It's a journey*. Let's understand this with a simple analogy. How do I travel to Dubai from Delhi? The answer is simple: I buy the air tickets. Now why would I want to travel to Dubai? Obviously, there has to be a purpose to my journey. The purpose could be a business trip, a vacation, visiting relatives, or to explore. Do you think I would buy the air tickets to Dubai and travel without a reason?

So, the point is that every journey has a purpose, and a clearly defined destination. And if life too is a journey, then there has to be a purpose to this journey and a clearly defined destination. There is a reason for our existence if we do not have a purpose.

> ***'There are two most important days in a person's life: the day they are born and the day they know why.'***
>
> ***– Mark Twain***

Who are the most successful people in the world? They are the people who are doing what they want to do. They have thriving businesses or they are busy doing whatever it is that they love. They have the time and energy to do the things that they love, both at work and outside it. Success is more than just material possessions. It is about getting to live the life that you love and love the life that you live. It's a 360-degree experience, which gives meaning to your life and makes you feel deeply alive.

The most successful people in the world have discovered (consciously or unconsciously) their 'why', the reason for their existence.

This *why* is the purpose of your life.

What do most people do today when they have to decide what they want to be or do in life? What is important to them?

Most of us let the external world dictate what is important for us – what we should set as our goals, which is in most of the cases is money and fame. A survey by the Pew Research Centre in 2007 revealed that young people (18–25 years old) placed wealth and fame as their two main goals.

It's no different for most of us. We choose not to listen to our inner guiding voice, our intuition. This is the voice of our dreams. Our dream is where our passion lies. Our dream is that for which our heart craves.

It is thus sensible to stop the noise from the external world and be in silence in order to listen to the inner voice, the voice of your heart – to find out what you really want to do in life.

Your purpose is simply to discover, pursue, and realize your dream and unwrap the gift lying within and then share it with the world.

A lot of people don't know their purpose and if you don't know your purpose, your immediate goal is to figure that out, otherwise you are on autopilot, wandering like a sailing boat drifting endlessly in the open ocean with no direction. A sailboat such as that is destined to perish. The sooner you can figure out what it is that you are supposed to be doing, the sooner you will start working towards achieving that. However, the challenge for many people is to find their purpose in life, to find out what they are passionate about.

How do you figure out what is your purpose in life?

Your purpose in life will always be something you love doing or something you have always dreamt of doing. It's your real calling. It will be something that you would do happily

24/7 and never get tired. Your purpose will be something or a combination of things that would constantly inspire you and lead you forward, regardless of the setbacks and challenges you might face.

Remember you are special and unique. No one can think and feel just like you. You have uniqueness within you and your purpose is to find that uniqueness and share it with the world.

In a nutshell, your purpose is your *passion*, your *dream*. It is something that you have fallen in love with and really want. All successful people are doing what they are passionate about. It's so much easier to endure, overcome challenges and keep going if your goals are set with passion.

Richard St John, a success expert and an author, interviewed over 500 successful millionaires and billionaires all over the world over a ten-year-long survey. He found that none of them had fame and fortune as their primary goals in life. They all came from passion.

These people don't focus on the money; it comes anyway. They didn't chase after the money or fame, all of that followed as a bonus. These people had found their *purpose*. These people followed their hearts, they followed their dreams, and they let their dreams have them completely.

I believe that each of us is born with a purpose in life. Identifying, acknowledging, and honouring this purpose is perhaps the most important action that successful people take. They take the time to understand what they're here to do – and then they pursue that with passion and enthusiasm.

Now I want to ask you this question:

- *What is your 'why'? Have you discovered your 'why'? The day you do is the second-most important day of your life.*

I call it the second-birth. I felt reborn when I discovered my 'why'. So, how do you find this 'missing piece' of your life? I am sure you know by now. Yes! By asking the right questions. So, here are a few powerful questions that will help you discover your passion, your purpose. I suggest you take one question at a time, think and write the answers:

- ***What do you love to do?*** Your purpose is related to what you love doing, so write down all the activities that you love. Sachin Tendulkar loves playing cricket. Amitabh Bachchan loves acting. Write down as many things as you can. Your 'why' is hidden somewhere here.
- ***What grabs you attention when it's not functioning properly?*** For instance, a fashion designer would immediately notice if you have committed a fashion mistake. So, whatever it is for you, just write it down.
- ***What do you love to learn about?***
- ***What do you love to talk about?***
- ***What would you regret never trying?***
- ***What are you good at? What sparks your creativity?***

Now, take a moment and review all the answers that you have written. What are the commonalities? Write them down.

Next, make a list of all the career, job or business opportunities that someone with this passion would pursue. There would be something on this list that you feel the most passionate about doing, one that seems the most enticing to you, one that you can see yourself doing forever, one that deep down inside you believe you can do, one that you won't regret trying. Mark it on this list.

This exercise is a very powerful way to discover your purpose. I can say this with confidence because I have used it myself and with many people that I work with. However, sometimes it takes time to reveal itself. People often ask me, why is this 'why' not revealed easily? Why is this 'why' so elusive?

My answer: The purpose reveals itself to us only when we are ready for it.

Ready for it? What do you mean by that?

Yes, most of us are not ready for it. The majority of people are not even aware of this most important piece of their life. As I always say, awareness is the first step towards creating change. Only when we are aware that we are all born for a purpose and realize that we need to evolve and grow as a person, who then would be able to pursue that purpose, will that 'why' reveal itself. That's what the intention of this book was: to prepare you to get you ready to explore your real calling, your 'why'.

Your purpose will automatically reveal itself to you when you become the person who is ready to know his/her purpose and work towards achieving it. This is the law of the universe. When you are ready to ask, you shall receive. When you are ready to receive, you shall get. When you are ready to seek, you shall find.

Taking you through these powerful ideas to set you on the path to success has been an amazing journey for me. I can say with certainty that if you work on implementing these ideas in your life, your life will never be the same again. I will conclude this beautiful journey with a simple question for you:

Are you READY?

AUTHOR'S NOTE

The stories mentioned in the book are based on real life incidents. The names of my clients and acquaintances have been purposely changed.

ACKNOWLEDGEMENTS

Great accomplishments happen only when you have a team of some brilliant people to make these possible. The publishing of this book is no exception.

I offer my sincerest gratitude to His Divine Grace Sarv Shri Ashutosh Maharaj Ji whose teachings and spiritual guidance have been the very foundation of my existence. He has been and continues to be my inspiration and my role model in living a life of integrity and strong character. He has been the sole reason behind the writing of this book. As he says, 'If you want to make this world a better place, share your knowledge and lessons with as many people as possible.' What better way to do this than to spread the knowledge with a book!

My husband, Vipin, and son, Keshav, have provided me support, assistance, and encouragement, right from the conception of this book. Without them, this book would have been only a dream and I cannot thank them both enough for everything that they have done for me in making it a reality.

My deepest gratitude to my spiritual brother, Swami Vishalanand who stood by me when I needed him the most

Special thanks to Mr Sandip Das for being an incredible guide and for writing the foreword of the book.

My heartfelt thanks to Arfeen Khan, for being a powerful mentor and guide to me.

I am also grateful to Ms Padmini Smetacek, whose editorial expertise made my work look and sound so much better.

My sincere thanks to Avneet Kaur for helping me fine-tune and shape the book the way it looks today and to the Pan Macmillan India team for making this book a reality.

A special thanks to my clients and participants who allowed me to share their stories, which has helped in making this work so relatable.

A BIG thank you to my parents, my in-laws, my siblings and friends, whose love, support and blessings have made this journey so beautiful.

A special mention to all the viewers who follow my work online. I consider you all my extended family and you have been an inspiration to me.

And thanks to you – my reader – for giving me an opportunity to share my work and wisdom with you.

NOTES

INTRODUCTION

1. 'Mind, Growth, and Matter.' Bruce Lipton. Succeed Magazine, June 7, 2012. https://www.brucelipton.com/resource/interview/mind-growth-and-matter.

2. van Rensburg, Mae. 'A Child's Subconscious Mind: How Parents Can Hurt or Help Their Kids.' AAP Medianet. Accessed October 21, 2019. https://www.medianet.com.au/releases/128343/.

CHAPTER 2: THE UNSTOPPABLE POWER OF DECISIONS

1. Camp, Jim. 'Decisions Are Largely Emotional, Not Logical: the Neuroscience behind Decision-Making.' Big Think. Big Think, January 4, 2019. https://bigthink.com/experts-corner/decisions-are-emotional-not-logical-the-neuroscience-behind-decision-making.

2. Barb, and Gilda. "Science of the Heart.' HeartMath Institute, February 24, 2017. https://www.heartmath.org/research/science-of-the-heart/.

CHAPER 3: FAILURE IS YOUR HIGHWAY TO SUCCESS

1. Flood, Alison. 'JK Rowling Says She Received "Loads" of Rejections before Harry Potter Success.' *The Guardian*. Guardian News and Media, March 24, 2015. https://www.theguardian.com/books/2015/mar/24/jk-rowling-tells-fans-twitter-loads-rejections-before-harry-potter-success.

CHAPTER 6: INVESTING IN TAKING RISKS IN LIFE

1. Feifer, Jason. 'Richard Branson on the Importance of Taking Meaningful Risks'. *Entrepreneur*, October 26, 2017. https://www.entrepreneur.com/article/302033.

CHAPTER 7: CLARITY OF VISION

1. Tony, Team. 'Energy Flows Where Attention Goes - Focus & Energy: Tony Robbins.' tonyrobbins.com, August 20, 2019. https://www.tonyrobbins.com/career-business/where-focus-goes-energy-flows/#targetText=As Tony Robbins says, energy flows where attention goes.&targetText=Once this is in place,your energy, amazing things happen.

CHAPTER 8: CREATING THE RIGHT ENVIRONMENT

1. Online, ET. 'Hire People Smarter than You, LQ Is Important: Quotes by Jack Ma to Help You Navigate Biz, Life.' *The*

Economic Times. Economic Times, September 10, 2019. https://economictimes.indiatimes.com/magazines/panache/hire-people-smarter-than-you-lq-is-important-quotes-by-jack-ma-to-help-you-navigate-biz-life/articleshow/71049140.cms?from=mdr.

2. Iny, Danny. 'How to Surround Yourself with the Right People (Even If You Can't Stand Your Relatives).' Inc.com. Inc., May 11, 2016. https://www.inc.com/danny-iny/how-to-surround-yourself-with-the-right-people-even-if-you-cant-stand-your-relat.html.

CHAPTER 9: BE A LIFELONG LEARNER

1. Simmons, Michael. 'Bill Gates, Warren Buffett And Oprah All Use The 5-Hour Rule.' *Medium*. Accelerated Intelligence, December 19, 2018. https://medium.com/accelerated-intelligence/bill-gates-warren-buffett-and-oprah-all-use-the-5-hour-rule-308f528b6363.

2. Rosman, Katherine. 'Bill Gates on Books and Blogging.' *The New York Times*. The New York Times, January 4, 2016. https://www.nytimes.com/2016/01/04/fashion/bill-gates-gates-notes-books.html.

3. Williams, Trey. 'Mark Zuckerberg Resolves to Read a Book Every Other Week in 2015.' MarketWatch, January 5, 2015. https://www.marketwatch.com/story/mark-zuckerberg-resolves-to-read-a-book-every-other-week-in-2015-2015-01-05.

4. ZamTheWriter. 'Billionaire Elon Musk Says He Was "Raised by Books" and Credits His Success to These 8.' CNBC. CNBC, November 16, 2017. https://www.cnbc.com/2017/11/16/tesla-ceo-elon-musk-says-he-was-raised-by-books.html.

5. 'The Global Council on Brain Health (GCBH).' AARP. Accessed October 23, 2019. https://www.aarp.org/health/brain-health/global-council-on-brain-health/.

6. Andrews, Robin. 'Regularly Reading Books Prolongs Your Life By Up To Two Years.' *IFLScience*. IFLScience, September 12, 2019. https://www.iflscience.com/brain/regularly-reading-books-prolongs-life-two-years/.

7. Andrews, Robin. 'Regularly Reading Books Prolongs Your Life By Up To Two Years.' *IFLScience*. IFLScience, September 12, 2019. https://www.iflscience.com/brain/regularly-reading-books-prolongs-life-two-years/.

8. Sophia, Team The Wisdom Post. 'Top 10 Success Principles to Learn from Jack Ma.' *The Wisdom Post*, January 23, 2018. http://www.thewisdompost.com/billionaires/jack-ma/top-10-success-principles-learn-jack-ma/1759.

CHAPTER 11: THE GIFT OF EMOTIONAL MASTERY

1. 'Loneliness Is a Major Health Risk for Older Adults.' ScienceDaily, ScienceDaily, 16 Feb. 2014, https://www.sciencedaily.com/releases/2014/02/140216151411.htm.

CHAPTER 12: THE IRRITABILITY CURE

1. 'Understanding Anger by Smitha Abraham.' Boloji.com, https://www.boloji.com/articles/3240/understanding-anger.

CHAPTER 13: PROCRASTINATION: BAD OR GOOD?

1. 'Behavior, Motivation and Self-Control.' Psychological Self-Help, https://www.psychologicalselfhelp.org/Chapter4.pdf.

CHAPTER 15: HOW TO HANDLE DIFFICULT PEOPLE

1. Cherry, Kendra. '5 Surprising Ways That Stress Affects Your Brain.' Verywell Mind. *Verywell Mind*, March 27, 2019. https://www.verywellmind.com/surprising-ways-that-stress-affects-your-brain-2795040.

2. 'Emotional Intelligence (EQ): The Premier Provider - Tests, Training, Certification, and Coaching.' TalentSmart. Accessed October 24, 2019. https://www.talentsmart.com/articles/How-Emotionally-Intelligent-People-Handle-Toxic-People-1028629190-p-1.html.

CHAPTER 18: ARE YOU MAKING THE MOST OF YOUR DIPS?

1. SpotboyE. 'Sanjay Dutt On Drug Overdose Days: "Mujhe Macchar Bhi Kaat Leta, Toh Woh Khudh Mar Jata."' Spotboye, June 29, 2018. https://spotboye.com/bollywood/news/sanjay-dutt-on-drug-overdose-days-mujhe-macchar-bhi-kaat-leta-toh-woh-khudh-mar-jata/5b34d4ed15c42201da4ca6ca.